Continuum Studies in
Research in Education

Series editor: Richard Andrews

Teaching and Learning English

D0771902

Related titles:

Martin Blocksidge (ed.): *Teaching Literature 11–18*
Manjula Datta: *Bilinguality and Literacy*
Andrew Goodwyn (ed.): *English in the Digital Age*
Diane Montgomery: *Spelling: Remedial Strategies*
Helen Nicholson (ed.): *Teaching Drama 11–18*

Teaching and Learning English

A guide to recent research and its applications

Richard Andrews

continuum
LONDON • NEW YORK

Continuum

The Tower Building 15 East 26th Street
11 York Road New York
London SE1 7NX NY 10010

www.continuumbooks.com

First published 2001

Reprinted 2005

British Library Cataloguing-in-Publication Data
A catalogue record for this book is available from the British Library.

ISBN   0–8264–5395–3 (hardback)
         0–8264–7738–0 (paperback)

Designed and typeset by Ben Cracknell Studios
Printed and bound in Great Britain by Antony Rowe Ltd., Chippenham, Wiltshire

Contents

Acknowledgements

No book of this kind can be written without extensive reference to the works of others. The following, in particular, have made their own contributions to the research underpinning English teaching.

I am grateful to Colin Harrison of the University of Nottingham for sending me the full report of his excellent evaluation of the Multimedia Portables for Teachers project and for allowing me to refer extensively to it in the chapter on ICT and English; to Lyn Fairfax at the National Association for the Teaching of English (Sheffield) for generously supplying me with back copies of *English in Education*; to Kathleen Tyner, Andy Goodwyn, Ilana Snyder, Wendy Morgan and Colin Lankshear for copies of their books; to Annah Levinovic-Healy for sending me a copy of her excellent thesis on reading in the post-typographic age; to Rebecca Sinker for sending me copies of her work, and to Sally Mitchell and Karen Raney for allowing me to quote from their research work; to the Universities of Hull and York for giving me time in the first six months of 2000 to complete my work on the book and to library staff at those universities and at the British Library, London, especially Kirstyn Radford at the J. B. Morrell Library of the University of York; to my children, David, Zoë and Grace, for allowing me to use their work in presentations that have contributed to the research in this book; to the editors of *English in Education* during the 1990s and up to the present: Ann Shreeve, Mark Reid, Margaret Wallen, Malcolm Kirtley, Julia Hodgeon, Richard Marshall, Geoff Barton; to key people in my own development as an English teacher: Geoffrey Summerfield, John Ferris, Ian Reid, Michael Simons, Stephen Clarke, Ian Bentley, Robert Protherough, Peter

Medway. Particular thanks go to Anthony Haynes at Continuum for his unstinting support and advice during the development of this title and of the series as a whole, and also to Alan Worth and Helen Power for their editorial contribution.

Some sections of this book appeared in earlier versions as reviews in *The European Journal of Teacher Education*. I am grateful to Maurice Whitehead for permission to reprint parts of reviews on books by Robin Peel, Annette Patterson, Jeanne Gerlach and Peter Benton. Part of Chapter 6 was first given as an inaugural professorial lecture at Middlesex University in 1995; parts of Chapter 7 were used in a keynote address at Middlesex University in July 2000 entitled 'Learning, Literacy and ICT: What's the Connection?', and thanks go to Shirley Franklin for the opportunity to address the conference 'Raising Standards across the Curriculum through Literacy and ICT at Key Stages 3 and 4'. Thanks must go, too, to the editors of the following journals for allowing research published therein to be cited: *English in Education, The English and Media Magazine, Educational Review* (UK), *Research in the Teaching of English* (USA), *Education, Communication & Information* (UK and USA), *English in Australia* and *Literacy Learning: Secondary Thoughts* (Australia).

Shortcomings in the book are my own. I would welcome responses which point out lacunae so that future editions might be improved.

Richard Andrews
York and New York, August 2000

Series Editor's Introduction

The function and role of the series

The need for the series

Internationally, the gap between research, policy and practice in public life has become a matter of concern. When professional practice – in nursing, education, local governance and other fields – is uninformed by research, it tends to reinvent itself in the light of a range of (often conflicting) principles. Research uninformed by practical considerations tends to be ignored by practitioners, however good it is academically. Similarly, the axis between policy and research needs to be a working one if each is to inform the other. Research is important to the professions, just as it is in industry and the economy: we have seen in the last fifteen years especially that companies which do not invest in research tend to become service agents for those companies that are at the cutting edge of practice. The new work order (see Gee *et al.*, 1996) makes research a necessity.

There is increasing interest in teaching as an evidence-based profession, though it is not always clear what an 'evidence-based profession' is. In the mid-1990s, in England, the Teacher Training Agency (TTA) was promoting a close link between research and the application of research in practice – for example, in the classroom. It also laid particular emphasis on teachers as researchers, seeming at the time to exclude university-based researchers from the picture. It quickly became evident, however, that research-based teaching was generally impracticable and often a diversion from the core business of teaching and learning. Furthermore, there was policy confusion as to whether the main thrust of the initiative was to encourage teachers to be researchers, or to encourage teachers to use research to improve their performance in the classroom. It is the second of these aims that gained in momentum during the late 1990s and the first part of the present century.

Teachers as users of research brought about a subtly different term: 'evidence-based practice' in an evidence-based profession. The analogy with developments in nursing education and practice were clear. David Hargreaves made the analogy in a keynote TTA lecture, speculating as to why the teaching profession was not more like the nursing and medical professions in its use of research. The analogy was inexact, but the message was clear enough: let researchers undertake education research, and let teachers apply it. With scarce resources and an increasing influence from the Department for Education and Employment (DfEE) in the formation and implementation of teachers' professional development following the 1988 paper *Teachers: Meeting the Challenge of Change*, the TTA's own position on evidence-based practice was limited and more focused. In 1999–2000 the agency initiated a series of conferences entitled 'Challenging teachers' thinking about research and evidence-based practice'. The DfEE's own paper *Professional Development* (2000) sets out for discussion the place of research within teachers' professional development, including the announcement of best practice research scholarships for serving teachers:

> We are keen to support teachers using and carrying out research, which is a valuable way to build knowledge and understanding about raising standards of teaching and learning. Research can have advantages for the individual teacher; for their school; and for other schools in sharing lessons learned. We believe that research can be a particularly valuable activity for experienced teachers. (p. 25)

Part of the function of the present series is to provide ready access to the evidence base for busy teachers, teacher-researchers, parents and governors in order to help them improve teaching which, in turn, will improve learning and raise standards. But it is worth discussing here what the evidence base is for teaching a school subject, and how it might be applied to the acts of teaching and learning.

Evidence is inert. It needs not so much application as *transformation* in order to make learning happen in the classroom. That transformation requires the teacher to weigh up the available evidence, devise pedagogical approaches to be included in an overall teaching programme for a year, term, week or unit of work and then to put those approaches into action. Evidence can inform both the planning and the actual delivery. Imagine yourself in the middle of teaching a class about differences between spoken standard English and a number of dialects. You can draw on the evidence to help you plan and teach the lesson, but you will also need to depend on the evidence in order to improvise, adapt and meet particular learning needs *during* the course of the lesson.

The gaps between policy, research and practice

In February 2000, in a possibly unprecedented gesture, the British Secretary of State for Education addressed a community of education researchers about the importance of its research for the development of government policy (DfEE, 2000). The basic message was that research, policy and practice needed to be in closer relation to each other in order to maximize the benefits of each. During the 1980s and 1990s, the gap between research and policy was chasm-like. Politicians and other policy-makers tended to choose research evidence to support their own prejudices about education policy. A clear case was the affirmation of the value of homework by successive governments in the face of research which suggested homework had little or no effect on the performance of pupils. Similarly, the gap between research and practice was often unbridged. One problem facing the education sector as a whole is that research moves to a different rhythm from policy or practice. Longitudinal research may take ten or fifteen years to gestate; policy moves in four-year cycles, according to governments and elections; practice is often interested in a short-term fix.

The creation of a National Education Research Forum in late 1999 goes some way to informing policy with research. Its function is very much to inform policy rather than to inform practice, and its remit is much larger than a focus on schooling. But its creation, along with the emergence of series such as the present one and websites which aim to mediate between research and practice can only improve the relationship between research, policy and practice. A virtuous triangle is slowly taking shape.[1]

The focus on subjects, at early years, primary/elementary and secondary/high school levels

The series is built around subjects. At the time of going to press, there are titles on English, Mathematics, Science, Design and Technology, Modern Foreign Languages and Economics and Business Studies either published or in the pipeline. Further titles will be added in due course. All but one of these subjects applies to primary/elementary and secondary/high school levels; one of the aims of the series is to ensure that research in the teaching and learning of school subjects is not confined by phase, but is applicable from the early years through to the end of compulsory education.

The focus on subjects is a pragmatic one. Although there is considerable pressure to move away from an essentially nineteenth-century conception of the curriculum as divided into disciplines and subjects, the current National Curriculum in England and Wales, and curricula elsewhere in the world, are still largely designed on the basis of subjects. The research we have drawn on in the making of the present series therefore derives from the core discipline, the school subject and the teaching of the school subject in each case. Where other research is contributory to practice, we have not stopped at including it (for example the work of the social psychologist Vygotsky in relation to the teaching of English) so that each book is an interpretation by the author(s) of the significance of research to teaching and learning within the subject. With some subjects, the research literature is vast and the authors have made what they take to be appropriate selections for the busy teacher or parent; with other subjects, there is less material to draw on and the tendency has been to use what research there is, often carried out by the author or authors themselves.

We take it that research into the development of learning in a subject at primary school level will be of interest to secondary school teachers, and vice-versa. The books will also provide a bridge between phases of education, seeing the development of learning as a continuous activity.

The international range

The series is international in scope. It aims not only to draw on research undertaken in a range of countries across the world in order to get at the best evidence possible; it will also apply to different systems across the world because of its attempt to get at the bedrock of good teaching and learning. References to particular education systems are kept to a minimum, and are only used when it is necessary to illuminate the context of the research. Where possible, comparative research is referred to.

Such an international perspective is important for a number of reasons: first, because research is sometimes carried out internationally; second, because globalization in learning is raising questions about the basis of new approaches to learning; third, because different perspectives can enhance the overall sense of what works best in different contexts. The series is committed to such diversity, both in drawing on research across the world and in serving the needs of learners and teachers across the world.

The time frame for the research

In general, the series looks at research from the 1960s to the present. Some of the most significant research in some subjects was undertaken in the 1960s. In the 1990s, the advent of the Internet and the World Wide Web has meant that the research toolkit has been increased. It is now possible to undertake literature reviews online and via resources in formats such as CD-ROM, as well as via the conventional print formats of journals and books. The books cannot claim to be comprehensive; at the same time each is an attempt to represent the best of research in particular fields for the illumination of teaching and learning.

The nature of applied research in education

Applied research, as a term, needs some explication. It can mean both research into the application of 'blue-skies' research, theory or ideas in the real-world contexts of the classroom or other site of education and learning; and it can also mean research that arises from such contexts. It sometimes includes action research because of the close connection to real-world contexts. It is distinctly different from desk-based research, 'blue-skies' research or research into the history, policy or socio-economics of education as a discipline. There is further exploration of different kinds of research in the next section. Here I want to set out why applied research cannot be fully disconnected from other kinds of research, and to demonstrate the unity and inter-connectedness of research approaches in education.

Research has to be 'academic' in the sense of the *disinterested* pursuit of truth (to the extent that truth is an absolute). If the research does not attempt to be as objective as it can be (within the paradigm within which it adopts – which may be a subjective one), it cannot be taken seriously.

Second, research – like practice – has to be informed by theory. There is little point in undertaking action research or empirical research without a clear sense of its underlying assumptions and ideologies. Theory, too, needs to be examined to ensure that it supports or challenges practice and convention. The crucial point in the present response is that a research cycle may require full treatment of each of the following phases of research:

- definition of the problem or research question; or positing of a hypothesis;
- review of the theory underpinning the field or fields in which the empirical research is to be undertaken;
- devising of an appropriate methodology to solve the problem, answer the research question or test the hypothesis;
- empirical work with qualitative and/or quantitative outcomes;
- analysis and discussion of results;
- conclusion; and implications for practice and further research.

The stages of conventional research, outlined above, might be undertaken as part of a three-year full-time or five- to six-year part-time research degree; or they might form the basis of an action research cycle (at its simplest, 'plan–do–review'). Although the cycle as a whole is important, research is not invalidated if it undertakes one or more stages or elements of the cycle. For example, research which undertook to cover the first two stages in a thorough examination of the literature on a particular topic could be very useful research; similarly, research which aimed to test an existing theory (or even replicate an earlier study in a new context) – the fourth, fifth and sixth stages as outlined above – might also be very useful research.

It is a mistake to think that research must be immediately applicable. If we think of the most influential research of the last thirty years – Barnes *et al.*'s work on talk in classrooms in the late 1960s for example – we would note in this case that its impact might not be felt fully until fifteen years later (in the introduction of compulsory testing of oral competence in English (in England and Wales) in 1986).

In short, a large cycle over a number of years can be as important (it is often more so) than a short action research cycle over a year or two. We do need further research into how teachers actually change and improve their practice before we can make too many assumptions about the practical value of research.

Different kinds of research

Different kinds of research can be identified. They are:

1. theoretical, historical and strategic research;
2. applied research (including evaluation, consultancy);
3. research for and about learning;
4. scholarship.

These categories are not perfect; categories rarely are. Nor are they exclusive.

Theoretical, historical and strategic research

These kinds of research, along with strategic research, do not have immediate practical application. Their importance is undiminished in the light of a gradual shift towards the impact of research and the presence of 'users' on Research Assessment Exercise panels.[2] In the 1990s, there was a gradual widening of the definition of research to include artefacts and other patentable inventions.

The following definition of research is both catholic and precise:

'Research' for the purpose of the research assessment exercise is to be understood as original investigation undertaken in order to gain knowledge and understanding. It includes work of direct relevance to the needs of commerce and industry, as well as to the public and voluntary sectors; scholarship; the invention and generation of ideas, images, performances and artefacts including design, where these lead to new or substantially improved insights; and the use of existing knowledge in experimental development to produce new or substantially improved materials, devices, products and processes, including design and construction. It excludes routine testing and analysis of materials, components and processes, e.g. for the maintenance of national standards, as distinct from the development of new analytical techniques. It also excludes the development of teaching materials that do not embody original research. (HEFCE, 1998)

Applied research, including evaluation and consultancy

Much research may be of an applied kind. That is to say, it might include:

- research arising from classroom and school needs;
- research undertaken in schools, universities and other workplaces;
- research which takes existing knowledge and applies or tests it in different contexts;
- research through knowledge and technology transfer;
- collaborations with industry, other services (e.g. health), arts organizations and other bodies concerned with improving learning and the economy in the region and beyond;
- evaluation;
- consultancies that include a research dimension; and
- the writing of textbooks and other works designed to improve learning, as long as these textbooks are underpinned by research and there is evidence of such research.

The common factor in these approaches is that they are all designed to improve learning in the different fields in which they operate, and thus to inform teaching, training and other forms of education.

Research for and about learning and teaching

Research into the processes of learning is often interdisciplinary. It might include:

- fundamental enquiry into learning processes;
- research into a region's educational needs;
- the creation of a base of applied research to underpin professional practice;
- the establishment of evidence for the provision of specific pedagogic materials;

- the development of distance-learning techniques, materials and modes of delivery; and
- examination of cases of cutting-edge learning.

Research *for* learning means research designed to improve the quality of learning; in some quarters, it is referred to as 'research and development' ('R&D'). It is a well-known and well-used approach in the making of new products. The writing of school textbooks and other forms of publication for the learning market, whether in print or electronic form, qualifies as research for learning if there is evidence of research under-pinning it. Such research is valuable in that it works towards the creation of a new product or teaching programme.

Research *about* learning is more conventional within academic research cultures. It is represented in a long-standing tradition with the cognitive sciences, education, sociology and other disciplines. Education research does and should cover learning in informal and formal settings. Research for learning should be grounded in research about learning.

Scholarship

Scholarship can be defined as follows: 'scholarship [is] defined as the creation, development and maintenance of the intellectual infrastructure of subjects and disciplines, in forms such as dictionaries, scholarly editions, catalogues and contributions to major research databases' (HEFCE, 1998). But there is more to scholarship than this. As well as supporting and maintaining the intellectual infrastructure of subjects and disciplines, scholarship is a practice and an attitude of mind. It concerns the desire for quality, accuracy and clarity in all aspects of learning; the testing of hunches and hypotheses against rigorous evidence; the identification of different kinds of evidence for different purposes (e.g. for the justification of the arts in the curriculum). It also reflects a quest for excellence in design of the written word and other forms of communication in the presentation of knowledge.

Teacher research

One aspect of the move to put research into the hands of its subjects or respondents has been the rise of practitioner research. Much of the inspiration for this kind of research has come from the work of Donald

Schön on the reflective practitioner (e.g. Schön, 1987) in the 1980s. Practitioner research puts the practitioner centre stage and in its purest form the research is directed, undertaken and evaluated by the practitioners themselves. In less pure forms, it is facilitated by outside researchers who nevertheless make sure that the needs and ideas of the practitioners are central to the progress of the research. Teacher research or 'teachers as researchers' is one particular manifestation of this movement. Key books are those by Webb (1990) and Webb and Vulliamy (1992).

The advantages of teacher research are that it is usually close to the concerns of the classroom, its empirical work is carried out in the classroom and the benefits of the research can be seen most immediately in the classroom. Most often it takes the form of action research, with the aim of improving practice. When the research is of a rigorous nature, it includes devices such as pre-test (a gauging of the state of play before an experiment is undertaken), the experimental period (in which, for example, a new method of teaching a particular aspect of a subject is tried) and post-test (a gauging of the state of play at the end of the experimental period). Sometimes more scientifically based approaches, like the use of a control group to compare the effects on an experimental group, are used. Disadvantages include the fact that unless such checks and balances are observed, the experiments are likely to become curriculum development rather than research, with no clear means of evaluating their value or impact. Furthermore, changes can take place without a sense of what the state of play was beforehand, or how far the changes have had an effect. Grass-roots projects like the National Writing Project and National Oracy Project in England and Wales in the late 1980s were of this nature: they tended to embrace a large number of practitioners and to be pursued with much enthusiasm; but at the end of the day, the community as a whole was none the wiser about the effect or impact of the innovations.

In the second half of the 1990s, the TTA in England and Wales initiated two programmes that gave more scope for teachers to undertake research themselves rather than be the users or subjects of it. The Teacher Research Grant Scheme and the School-Based Research Consortia enabled a large number of teachers and four consortia to undertake research. Much of it is cited in this series, and all of it has been consulted. Not all this kind of research has led to masters or doctoral work in universities, but a larger number of teachers have undertaken dissertations and theses across the world to answer research questions and test hypotheses about aspects of education. Again, we have made every effort to track down and represent research of this kind. One of the criticisms made by the TTA in the late 1990s was that much of this latter academic research was neither applicable nor was applied to the classroom. This criticism may have arisen from a misunderstanding about the scope, variety and nature of education research, discussed in the section on the nature of applied research above.

The applicability of academic research work to teaching

This section deals with the link between masters and doctoral research, as conducted by students in universities, and its applicability to teaching. The section takes question-and-answer format.[3] The first point to make is about the nature of dissemination. Dissemination does not only take place at the end of a project. In many projects (action research, research and development) dissemination takes place along the way, for example in networks that are set up, databases of contacts, seminars, conferences and in-service education. Many of these seminars and conferences include teachers (e.g. subject professional conferences).

What arrangements would encourage busy education departments, teacher-researchers and their colleagues to collaborate in the dissemination of good quality projects likely to be of interest and use to classroom teachers? What would make teachers enthusiastic about drawing their work to the attention of colleagues?

Good dissemination is partly a result of the way a research project is set up. Two examples will prove the point: one from the University of Hull and one from Middlesex University.

Between 1991 and 1993 an action research project was undertaken by the University of Hull's (then) School of Education to improve the quality of argument in ten primary and ten secondary schools in the region. Teachers collaborated with university lecturers to set up mini-projects in each of the schools. These not only galvanized interest among other teachers in each of the schools, but made for considerable exchange between the participating schools. Much dissemination (probably reaching at least two hundred teachers in the region) took place *during* the project. Conventional *post hoc* dissemination in the form of articles and presentations by teachers took place after the project.

In early 1998, Middlesex University, through the TTA's inservice education and training (INSET) competition, won funding in collaboration with the London Boroughs of Enfield and Barnet to run INSET courses from September 1998. Alongside the INSET courses themselves, four MPhil/PhD studentships were awarded for teachers to undertake longer-term evaluations of in-service curricular development. At the time (September 1998) several applicants wished to focus their research on the literacy hour. This research informed INSET activity and was of interest to teachers in the region, as well as providing summative evidence for a wider community.

In conclusion, the research projects of relevance to teachers must a) be engaging, b) be disseminated during the course of the research as well as after it, c) be seen to benefit schools during the research as well as after it, and d) involve as large a number of teachers in the activity of the project as possible. Diffidence about research is not felt if there is involvement in it.

How can we encourage more pedagogic research with a focus on both teaching and learning?

Research into learning often has implications for teaching; and it is difficult in disciplined research to have two foci. Indeed such bifocal research may not be able to sustain its quality. Inevitably, any research into teaching must take into account the quality and amount of learning that takes place as a result of the teaching. Research into *learning* is again a pressing need. Having said that, research with a focus on *teaching* needs to be encouraged.

Would it be beneficial to build a requirement for accessible summaries into teacher research programmes? Given the difficulties involved in this process, what training or support would be needed by education researchers?

The ability to summarize is an important skill; so is the ability to write accessibly. Not all teachers or teacher researchers (or academics for that matter) have such abilities. We do not see such a requirement to be problematical, however, nor to need much attention. Teacher researchers must simply be required to provide accessible summaries of their work, whether these are conventional abstracts (often no longer than 300 words) or longer summaries of their research. Their supervisors and the funding agency must ensure that such summaries are forthcoming and are well written.

Where higher degree study by teachers is publicly funded, should teachers be required to consider from the start how their work might involve colleagues and be made accessible to other teachers?

Making a researcher consider from the start how their work might involve colleagues and be made accessible to other teachers is undesirable for a number of reasons. First, it might skew the research. Second, it will put the emphasis on dissemination and audience rather than on the research itself. Part of the nature of research is that the writer must have his or her focus on the material gathered or the question examined, not on what he or she might say. This is why writing up research is not necessarily like writing a book; a thesis must be true to its material, whereas a book must speak to its audience. There is a significant difference in the two genres, which is why the translation of thesis into book is not always as easy as it might seem. Third, what is important 'from the start' is the framing of a clear research question, the definition of a problem or the positing of a testable hypothesis.

In summary, as far as teacher research and the use of findings in MA and PhD work go, there are at least the following main points which need to be addressed:

- further research on how teachers develop and improve their practice;
- exploration and exposition of the links between theory and practice;
- an understanding that dissemination is not always most effective 'after the event';
- an appreciation of the stages of a research project, and of the value of work that is not immediately convertible into practice;
- further exploration of the links between teaching and learning.

Research is not the same as evaluation

It is helpful to distinguish between research and evaluation for the purposes of the present series. Research is the critical pursuit of truth or new knowledge through enquiry; or, to use a now obsolete but nevertheless telling definition from the eighteenth century, research in music is the seeking out of patterns of harmony which, once discovered, can be applied in the piece to be played afterwards. In other words, research is about discovery of new patterns, new explanations for data – or the testing of existing theories against new data – which can inform practice.

Evaluation is different. One can evaluate something without researching it or using research techniques. But formal evaluation of education initiatives often requires the use of research approaches to determine the exact nature of the developments that have taken place or the value and worth of those developments. Evaluation almost always assumes critical detachment and the disinterested weighing up of strengths and weaknesses. It should always be sensitive to the particular aims of a project and should try to weigh the aims against the methods and results, judging the appropriateness of the methods and the validity and effect (or likely effect) of the results. It can be formative or summative: formative when it works alongside the project it is evaluating, contributing to its development in a critical, dispassionate way; and summative when it is asked to identify at the end of a project the particular strengths and weaknesses of the approach.

Evaluation can use any of the techniques and methods that research uses in order to gather and analyse data. For example, an evaluation of the strengths and weaknesses of the TTA's School-Based Research Consortia could use formal questionnaires, semi-structured interviews and case studies of individual teachers' development to assess the impact of the consortia. Research methods that provide quantitative data (largely numerical) or qualitative data (largely verbal) could be used.

Essentially, the difference between research and evaluation comes down to a difference in function: the function of research is to discover new knowledge via a testing of hypothesis, the answering of a research question or the solving of a problem – or indeed the creation of a hypothesis, the asking of a question or the formulating or exploring of a problem. The function of evaluation is simply to evaluate an existing phenomenon.

How to access, read and interpret research

The series provides a digest of the best and most relevant research in the teaching and learning of school subjects. Each of the authors aims to mediate between the plethora of research in the field and the needs of the busy teacher, headteacher, adviser, parent or governor who wants to know how best to improve practice in teaching in order to improve standards in learning. In other words, much of the work of seeking out research and interpreting it is done for you by the authors of the individual books in the series.

At the same time, the series is intended to help you to access and interpret research more generally. Research is continuing all the time; it is impossible for a book series, however comprehensive, to cover all research or to present the very latest research in a particular field. The publisher and authors of individual titles will be happy to hear from readers who feel that a particular piece of research is missing from the account, or about new research that extends our understanding of the field.

In order to help you access, read and interpret research the following guidelines might help:

- How clear is the research question or problem or hypothesis?
- If there is more than one question or problem, can you identify a main question or problem as opposed to subsidiary ones? Does the researcher make the distinction clear?
- Is any review of the literature included? How comprehensive is it? How critical is it of past research? Does it, for instance, merely cite previous literature to make a new space for itself? Or does it build on existing research?
- Determine the size of the sample used in the research. Is this a case study of a particular child or a series of interviews with, say, ten pupils, or a survey of tens or hundreds of pupils? The generalizability of the research will depend on its scale and range.
- Is the sample a fair reflection of the population that is being researched? For example, if all the 12- to 13-year-old pupils in a particular town are being researched (there might be 600 of them), what is the size of the sample?
- Are the methods used appropriate for the study?
- Is the data gathered appropriate for an answering of the question, testing of the hypothesis or solving of the problem?
- What conclusions, if any, are drawn? Are they reasonable?
- Is the researcher making recommendations based on sound results, or are implications for practice drawn out? Is the researcher aware of the limitations of the study?
- Is there a clear sense of what further research needs to be undertaken?

Equipped with questions like these, and guided by the authors of the books in the series, you will be better prepared to make sense of research findings and apply them to the improvement of your practice for the benefit of the students you teach. The bibliographies at the end of each book (or of individual chapters) will provide you with the means of exploring the field more extensively, according to your own particular interests and needs.

Richard Andrews

Notes

1   The creation of this Evidence-Informed Policy and Practice Initiative (EPPI) in 2000, based at the Institute of Education, has been a significant step forward. Six review groups, including one on English based at The University of York, were set up initially to conduct systematic reviews in the field.

2   The Research Assessment Exercise, conducted by the Higher Education Funding Council For England, was undertaken at four or five-year intervals between 1986 and 2001 and may or may not take place in the middle of the first decade of the century. Its aim is to gauge the quality of research produced by research institutions around the UK in order to attribute funding in subsequent years. Critics of the exercise have suggested that, despite attempts to make it recognize the value of applied research and the applicability of research, its overall effect has been to force departments of education in universities to concentrate on producing high quality research rather than working at the interface of research and practice.

3   This section is based on a submission by the author to the TTA in 1998.

Chapter 1

What is English?

Definitions of English

Imagine a typical English class in a primary or secondary school in the first decade of the twenty-first century, and compare it with a similar class of, say, twenty-five years ago. The class of the late 1970s or (very) early 1980s would have had no computer accessible to the pupils. Work would be essentially literature based, with language exercises emerging from an engagement with literature. There might be group work as well as teacher-controlled discourse, and an increasing emphasis on the value of talk in the classroom. In short, practice would have been socially based, with writing gradually freeing itself from the dualistic confines of two-tier examination systems at sixteen and an awareness of the potential of a wider world of discourse being explored.

In contrast, the English classroom of the 2000s is notable for a number of changes. Before we list these typical changes, however, let us acknowledge what has not changed. There is still a classroom with roughly the same number of young people in it. Teachers still plan and execute lessons. There is probably about the same proportion of class-taught and group-work activity. In terms of pedagogy and immediate context, not much has changed. But there is less dependence on literature as the foundation for the subject's practices, more differentiation, a more tightly planned sense of potential learning outcomes, more assessment and, in many places in the world, a national curriculum framework or equivalent within which the teacher and pupils are working. Literacy has been more clearly distinguished from

'English', and there is the presence of at least one computer in the classroom, with more around the school for teacher and pupil use. In short, pupils work a little more individualistically in a more controlled environment than in 1980, with a wider range of discourses and media at their disposal.

This book covers research underpinning the teaching and learning of English at primary and secondary levels in schooling during this period; that is to say, it embraces a subject that appears at elementary or primary levels as 'literacy', 'new literacies', or 'language arts' and at secondary or high-school levels as English. The first chapter addresses the question of 'English' itself, a question that Peel *et al.* (2000) have described as 'narcissistic' but which, nevertheless, must be addressed at the beginning of a book that purports to cover research underpinning the subject. The second chapter turns its attention more specifically to speaking and listening, followed by a third on writing. Completing the focus on what has been considered the core of the subject, the fourth chapter looks at reading – including reading difficulties. Chapter 5 focuses on literature teaching. It is Chapters 6 and 7 that recognize that new ground has been broken in the last ten to fifteen years: the territories of still and moving images on the one hand, and information and communication technologies on the other. While these two are not unrelated, they deserve separate chapters in that the widening of 'English' to embrace them raises new and different questions about practice in the classroom and about the English curriculum. What the book does not cover is English as a second or foreign language, bilingual education (except for passing reference) or an extensive look at university-level English. The conception of the subject at higher education level is important, however, for the backwash effect on curricula at 16–19 and thence on to the compulsory school years.

The terminology of the field is itself interesting. Bergonzi (1990), in his review of the state of English as a discipline at university level, ends with a bleak prospect:

> The most likely future is no overt change, with the discipline of English becoming less and less coherent, riven by feuds and revolts, but still presenting the external appearances of a large, well-established and respectable academic subject. It could go on for a long time in this condition, like the Spanish Empire in its centuries of decline. (p. 204)

The tone of wry resignation in those sentences, written after a decade of postmodernist raids and attacks on the discipline, indicates the weariness in a book which charts the exploding, fragmenting nature of English. At secondary level, at least for examination purposes at 16 and 18 in England, there is some protection from the territorial uncertainties of academic study in that the subject is divided into 'English Language' and 'English Literature'. Lower down the secondary school (ages 11–14) the subject unifies into 'English', and then at primary levels, what used to be called 'Language' is now referred to as 'Literacy', with an emphasis on acquiring the basic skills being at the top of government agendas in education. Further still, the emphasis is on reading, with writing being assumed to emerge from an engagement with a range of genres and forms in one's reading.

Another difference in the stages of English is that speaking and listening figure in the compulsory schooling years as part of the subject, though in descending priority order of reading, writing, speaking and listening. At university level, practice or theory in speaking and listening is very rare as part of the study of English, except in Linguistics and in pedagogical approaches to the teaching of literature.

There are other issues to consider about the nature of English. The first is that 'English' as a term locates the source of the subject (whether it includes the study of literature, other media and/or language) in the English language. To study English in, say, a school in Saudi Arabia or a university in Australia entails the cultural baggage that comes with the term. In its liberal versions, then, 'English' becomes a misnomer for what is actually being taught (e.g. literature in languages other than English, translations, Australian Media Studies). More conservatively, what looked like a simple solution to a core education in the classics at the beginning of the twentieth century – Sampson's proposals as couched in *English for the English* (1921) – looks overly simplistic at the beginning of the twenty-first. Bergonzi (1990) notes that any rational conception of the subject or discipline, based upon a comprehensive attempt at inclusion, would 'be unusably complex' (p. 76). 'English' might be the best umbrella term for the time being, but the subject is rapidly breaking out from under that umbrella.

One of two or three key marginal areas of the subject in the last quarter of the twentieth century has been Media Studies or Cultural Studies. Although offered at examination level in compulsory secondary schooling since the 1970s in England, these subjects have until recently failed to establish themselves as part of the mainstream curriculum in schools. Part of the reason is that the prevailing ideology behind the position of English in the curriculum has been one based on literature and personal development; another is that, since the 1980s, there has been an increasing emphasis on literacy and the teaching of basic skills within the subject. Marginal subjects like Media Studies have failed to establish themselves in the mainstream curriculum and have wavered between taking shelter under the umbrella of English – subsuming themselves in the process – or breaking out on their own and being consigned to marginal interests. Despite the growth in the popularity of Media Studies and related subjects at further education and degree level, the school picture still looks minimal and under-developed.

A breakthrough report, published in 1999 by the British Film Institute (Bazalgette, 1999), has begun to change the literature and personal development base of English, along with an emerging sense that literacy is no longer a monolithic print-bound phenomenon. There is further discussion of this pincer movement in Chapters 6 and 7, but here it is worth mentioning that the encroachment of moving image education on literariness combined with the awareness that young people are growing up in a world of multiple literacies, embodied most obviously on multimedia screens, are conspiring to change the conception of English. We are likely to see moving image education as well as the more static visual dimensions to literacy having a greater influence on the shape of the subject over the coming years.

The other curriculum area that is often subsumed within English is Drama. Again, this is an art-form and discipline in its own right. Like the other arts, Drama has had to fight its corner since the 1980s and has frequently taken refuge under the wing of English – often reluctantly. More recently, other art forms have been used by some education authorities to infuse the teaching of literacy, especially at primary/elementary school level where the curriculum is squeezed even more than at secondary level. What the arts gain from inclusion in the teaching of literacy or English is also lost in the disappearance of autonomy.

The emergence of English

John Dixon's *A Schooling in 'English'* (1991) presents interesting and convincing research on the emergence of the subject in the late nineteenth century. Taking his position in opposition to a number of 'cultural historians who counted themselves as radical critics but who

still based their work on unanalysed models and working assumptions'
(p. 3) – writers like Baldick (1983), Doyle (1989) and Eagleton (1983) –
he traces the beginnings of the subject to the extension classes organized
by women in the north of England in the 1860s. Far from being token
recognition on the part of universities at the time, Dixon traces the
vigorous arguments for the emerging subject in which working-class men
and women and men of the Co-operative Societies organized, attended
and paid for extension courses by university lecturers.

He also characterizes the emergence of the subject as identified by his
three points of reference. Eagleton saw the loss of ideological control by
the Victorian ruling class coinciding with 'the failure of religion' (1983:
22). Imaginative literature, according to Eagleton, offered 'an alternative
means of integrating social classes and exerting subtle forms of control
over the working masses' (Dixon, 1991: 4). Baldick (1983) shares Dixon's
understanding of the source of the subject, but sees the appropriation of
it by 'cultural superiors' in order to 'colonise' the working class, with the
aim of developing 'a new collective sense of Englishness' (p.19). Similarly,
Dixon characterizes Doyle's position as one that saw the enterprise of
English as part of a 'schedule for organizing the nation' (1983: 20).

Dixon's (1991) central thesis is that 'English' was primarily constituted
'in the activities jointly carried through by teachers and students – in
the oral and written dialogues they engage in' (p.7). These institutional
frames 'constrain and enable a particular set of possibilities for
understanding selves, groups and societies. And in order to do so, they
must include an analysis of specific types of dialogue, which mediate
and construct the way people act and relate' (p. 9). In other words, the
subject 'English' is constituted not so much by the texts that do or do
not make up its reading matter – the canon – but by the activities and
practices in exploring the relationship between text, teacher and student.
The subject is distinctive pedagogically in that it tries to draw out selves,
exploring their connection with wider societal, spiritual experiences via
imagination and critique.

Attitudes towards English

The Cox Report (Cox, 1989) identified five models of English teaching:

> It is possible to identify within the English teaching profession a
> number of different views on the subject. We list them here, though

we stress that they are not the only possible views, they are not sharply distinguishable, and they are certainly not mutually exclusive.

1. A 'personal growth' view focuses on the child: it emphasizes the relationship between language and learning in the individual child, and the role of literature in developing children's imaginative and aesthetic lives.
2. A 'cross-curricular' view focuses on the school: it emphasizes that all teachers have a responsibility to help children with the language demands of different subjects on the school curriculum . . .
3. An 'adult needs' view focuses on communication outside the school: it emphasizes the responsibility of English teachers to prepare children for the language demands of adult life, including the workplace, in a fast-changing world . . .
4. A 'cultural heritage' view emphasizes the responsibility of schools to lead children to an appreciation of those works of literature that have been widely regarded as amongst the finest in the language.
5. A 'cultural analysis' view emphasizes the role of English in helping children towards a critical understanding of the world and cultural environment in which they live. Children should know about the processes by which meanings are conveyed, and about the ways in which print and other media carry values.

Cox cautiously calls these 'views', and yet their power to influence the curricular shape of English and its application through teaching cannot be underestimated. In retrospect, one of the weaknesses of the Cox Report was that it simply described these different views and based its formulation of English upon 'good practice' without ever connecting the two. It operated on the assumption of an ideology-free 'best practice' model, its apparent ideology-free curriculum disguising the underpinning ideology that informed it, namely a combination of the first and fourth views above. It is not surprising that literature still held sway at the end of the twentieth century in a conception of English. It had done so since the 1920s, and Brian Cox's own predilections as a poet and Professor of English Literature at the University of Manchester coloured the dye.

A sixth model can now be added to those above, based on a 'digital literacy' view. As Richard Lanham (2001) points out, the core of text is now digital. Whether 'text' takes print or sonic or visual form (or a combination of these), the core remains digital. The effect of such a view is to reduce the dominance of print by raising the profile of electronic text, moving image and other forms of communication.

Both in articles in the 1990s (e.g. Goodwyn, 1992a; Goodwyn *et al.*, 1997) and in a recent book (Goodwyn, 2000a), Andrew Goodwyn has explored English teachers' views of English. He discovered that there 'is no doubt that [in 1992] personal growth [was] the most important model for the majority of teachers' in his sample of forty-six teachers (1992a: 6) and that 'it is also perceived as the most influential' (ibid.). Teachers were found to be confident about the literature base to their subject (perhaps reflecting the nature of their first degrees) but to be less confident about linguistics or other media, like film and video. They eschewed the responsibility for cross-curricular development of language skills and capabilities, preferring rather to see their role as developing children personally without much reference to the rest of the curriculum or to the outside world and 'adult needs'. There is also a suggestion in the results that English teachers still see themselves as educating children *against* the influence of popular media rather than helping them to 'read' a range of media; and that such an inoculatory approach to the teaching of the subject extended in the 1990s to protection against information and communication technology. Such defensiveness is on the decline, particularly in the light of the joint TTA and New Opportunities Fund initiative to train all serving teachers in the application of ICT in their subjects at primary and secondary levels by 2003. As Goodwyn and his co-writers say:

> The great majority of English teachers see the increasing presence of IT in English as inevitable and important, and they give an equal rating to its value for communication and for providing information . . . in [such a concept of literacy] electronic text plays a key part; it does not supplant print culture but it changes it. It includes more popular forms of reading and it is inclusive of television and video. It seems to us much closer to current practices of adult readers and more concerned with empowering readers than with transmitting a narrow view of 'being literate'. (1997: 60)

In a further, more extensive survey carried out in 1997, Goodwyn and Findlay (1999) report that by the end of the 1990s the attitude towards

English among English teachers was significantly different from that in the early 1990s. English teachers were opposed to the ideology underpinning the National Curriculum, seeing it as embodying notions of cultural heritage in an impersonal way – and not connecting to their still pre-eminent sense that English is about 'personal growth'. Whereas in 1991, teachers saw media education as only a small contributory part of English, by the late 1990s they were much more inclined to see it as an established part of the subject – despite the marginalization of it by the National Curriculum in the second half of the 1990s.

The trend, as identified by Tweddle (1995: 6), is towards a redefinition of 'the fundamental notion of text' (see also Lanham, 2001) 'and also of the range of activities defined as reading and writing'. This trend means that English will 'have at its heart the principle that literacy depends not on knowledge of specific texts but upon knowledge about texts' (p. 6). In this conception of English, and from the perspective of the first decade of the new century, the Kingman Report (Kingman *et al.*, 1988) on knowledge about language looks to have been a significant influence. It is a conception that grows out of a key article in the mid-1990s by Kress (1995) which sought to 'map out the terrain for the new debate' about English (p. 94). English as a subject or practice in the curriculum had a central role because of its capacity to provide us with 'the means of seeing ourselves as the makers of our means of making meaning' (ibid.) and a recognition of the developing and extending contexts in which English needs to be redefined, including multiculturalism, globalization and the 'changing landscape of communication' (ibid.). In a more recent review of the direction in which English is moving, Cliff Hodges *et al.* (2000) take up the baton, seeing English as increasingly drawing on notions or models of critical literacy (Morgan, 1996; Lankshear, 1997). This 'knowledge about texts' is at the heart of the debate about the kind of literacy that will be needed by young people as they grow up in the twenty-first century.

Literacy or literacies?

Though I will come back to the literacy debate in more detail in Chapters 3 and 4 on writing and reading respectively, it is worth rehearsing some of the issues that have driven the debate in recent years. One of the central conflicts, as Street (1997) and Wray (1997) point out, is that between those who see the grapho-phonemic[1] relationship as the basis of advancement in reading and those who favour a more organic, whole-text approach to literacy. These two positions are sometimes referred to as 'bottom-up' and 'top-down' approaches to the teaching of literacy. Understanding the nature of the debate and the way the various levels of language description relate to each other will be helped at this point with a table (see page 10).

Street (1997) points out that balanced approaches, which aim to combine grapho-phonemic and whole-text emphases, 'may not be as even-handed as the term suggests' (p. 46). Particular groups use a diction to persuade others of their point of view, claiming to introduce 'balance' by counteracting excesses by the other camp. In a particularly important message for readers of this book, he points out (p. 47) that claims like the TTA's (1997) which state that 'research shows' a phonic approach to be best and which blame falling standards of literacy on the strength of whole-language, meaning-based movements of the 1970s and 1980s are themselves highly partial accounts of the research literature. It is one thing to claim an underpinning in research; but such claims must be underpinned by a comprehensive review of the research rather than a selection from it.

The main drive of 'new literacy studies' or the 'new literacies' is to see language and literacy 'as social practices rather than technical skills to be learned in formal education' (Street, 1997: 47):

> The research requires language and literacy to be studied as they occur naturally in social life, taking account of the context and their different meanings for different cultural groups. The practice requires curriculum designers, teachers and evaluators to take account of the variation in meanings and uses that students bring from their home backgrounds to formal learning contexts. (ibid.)

Because new literacy studies accept that language is a dynamic, changing entity, the notion of multiple literacies follows. Rather than being seen as a fixed systematic 'literacy' that is replicable in different contexts, Street's conception is of a flexible, socially situated and diverse set of practices. This notion of a range of literacies – all positioning themselves in relation to power – is somewhat different from that of the New London Group (Cazden *et al.*, 1996; see below), who take the 'multi-' in 'multi-literacies' to mean the range of channels (print, visual, moving image, etc.) through which meaning is communicated. Street would prefer 'to think of literacies as some complex of these domains that

Level	Typical manifestation of teaching material at that level	Other issues and implications
Context	The social and/or political nature of texts; different kinds of context, ranging from the classroom to public contexts and real audiences on the one hand, to literary and linguistic contexts on the other	How contexts impact upon texts; the visual and/or multimedia context of the text in question; whether the text appears in print or on screen; the genesis and function of the text; the relationship of text to the still and moving image
Text	Issues of coherence and unity in literary and other texts; genre studies and applications; 'beginnings, middles and ends'; comparison of whole texts	The visual nature of the text; its purpose and function
Sub-units of text, e.g. paragraphs, stanzas	The shape and nature of sub-textual units; 'how to write a paragraph'; the structure of stanzas and verses in poetry	Issues of arrangement and rearrangement in the constituent parts of a text; sequencing
Sentence	Grammar teaching; 'parsing' of sentences; the combination of phrases in simple, compound and complex sentences	Questions about the definition of 'sentence'; questions as to whether teaching grammar explicitly is helpful in the development of literacy; sentence grammar as opposed to other grammars (e.g. speech grammars)
Phrase or clause	Grammatical rules	The efficacy or otherwise of teaching phrase and clause structure to native speakers and writers of the language
Word or lexical level	'Look and say' approaches; emphasis on the visual identification of spellings; etymologies	Word lists and their value; the study of dictionaries and thesauruses; the history of words
Morphological level	Using root words and morphological elements to teach spelling and reading	Arguments about the best ways to teach spelling and reading
Phonological level	More advanced phonetic approaches to spelling	Debates about the value of 'phonics' approaches to the teaching of reading
Grapho-phonemic level	'Phonetic' approaches to reading and spelling	Ditto
Alphabet	The nature, shape and sequence of the alphabet	History of writing; the emergence of the alphabet; use of dictionaries and other reference works based on alphabetic principles; visual representations of the alphabet in picture books and other sources (e.g. illuminated manuscripts)

varies with context, so that a mix of visual, print and other aspects depends upon cultural and contextual features' (1997: 49–50). He goes on: 'Computer literacy, for example, is not a new single literacy but involves different uses of oral and literate channels in different situations: there is no one phenomenon called "computer literacy" and the term can be misleading in both research and policy terms' (p. 50).

The particular charting of the landscape undertaken by Street and others (e.g. Freedman and Medway, 1994; Gee, 1991) which privileges a social reading of language description and development is helpful in getting to the heart of how language operates in society, both personally and politically. What this view tends to do is to break down language situations into particular occurrences which can then be described accurately from a sociolinguistic and/or anthropological or sociological perspective. Such analysis is necessary for a better understanding of how languages work in society, but it does not always translate readily into policy or practice, which tends to favour programmatic and pedagogical – and sometimes inspirational – *interventions* in order to improve language acquisition. It is a research-based rather than a practice- or policy-based approach.

A key article (Cazden *et al.*, 1996) points the way towards a different future for notions of literacy. The New London Group – so called after a meeting in New London, New Hampshire in 1994 – devised a concept of *multi*literacies. These are multifarious in that they reflect both the diversity of social situation in the world, increasingly widening at the present time, and also a multiplicity of channels through which communication takes place. The model is strong on the visual dimension of such literacies and sees design as the central concept 'in which we are both inheritors of patterns and conventions of meaning and at the same time active designers of meaning' (p. 65). In the spirit of multimedia communication, six design elements are discussed: linguistic, visual, audio, gestural, spatial and multimodal meaning, the latter relating the first five modes of meaning to each other. In terms of the social and political contexts which both shape and are affected by literacies, states (i.e. governments) 'must be strong as neutral arbiters of difference': the acceptance and/or resolution of difference, with the help of literacies, is a central project for education and schooling. Linguistic and cultural pluralism is at the heart of this model. There is much more in this article worth pursuing, and indeed it formed an early statement in an ongoing research project, the International Multiliteracies Project.

Such approaches to the widening of notions of literacy open up a theoretical window on possibilities like those reported in Brown *et al.* (1990) in which schools in the Leeds and Oldham areas in northern England experimented in the late 1980s with real-world writing that took the practice and development of literacy beyond the confines of the classroom to real audiences – with very positive effects for the students involved.

The Developing English for TVEI[2] project aimed to move English beyond its conventional literary territory into an engagement with 'real-world' situations. More specifically, the aim of the project was that 'the *language* promoted in English should go beyond the personal and the literary, to include the language of, for instance, decision-making, working in teams, making things happen, persuading people, helping people, organizing and informing, while the *content* of English should include people's experiences as contributors to economy and production, and the processes and products of their work, including technology' (ibid., p. 6). This extended notion of English did not intend to leave behind the literary; on the contrary, some of the most interesting writing to emerge from the project made a new fusion between the literary and the functional. For example, a 14-year-old student in Doncaster, who had visited a solicitor as part of a project to find out more about the world of work, wrote up her account in the following style:

> To be a solicitor takes a person who can work under extreme pressure and who has great personal organization. An image must be projected of sharp professionalism, Mr Burrow told us. The old-fashioned idea of the solicitor must be discarded: no more walking up endless rickety stairs to a dingy room full of dust and cobwebs. And so Mr Burrow led us up endless rickety stairs to a room full of dust and cobwebs. The shelves of files were eternal and the papers scattered everywhere. (p. 110)

Dickens meets Doncaster. Such projects have extended and enriched the lives of students and teachers, and also expanded our notion of what constitutes English.

The current state of English in the curriculum

The English curriculum in England has been the subject of intense debate, especially since the advent of the National Curriculum in the late 1980s.

This is not the place to rehearse again the twists and turns of policy between then and now. These are variously recorded in Andrews, 1996a; Barnes, 1993; Bousted, 1993; Clark, 1994; Dixon, 1994; Protherough, 1990 and 1993; Stratta and Dixon, 1992 and elsewhere. Rather, this book takes the 'lightly revised' National Curriculum of 2000 as its starting point (see DfEE, 1999a) and, while providing research underpinning for the delivery of the curriculum in schools over the coming years, also points out shortcomings of the curriculum in the light of research and charts a new curriculum for the subject.

The core requirements of the English curriculum cover speaking and listening, reading and writing: distinctive areas in themselves 'but since language development depends on their interrelatedness, teaching needs to build on the links between them' (DfEE, 1999a:6). What is missing is 'viewing', and we will return to that area in Chapter 6 of this book. English is also seen as promoting pupils' spiritual, moral, social and cultural development; as providing opportunities for pupils to develop the key skills of communication, capability with information technology, working with others, improving one's own learning and performance, and problem-solving. In particular, English is seen to have a role in promoting citizenship and thinking skills through:

- reading, viewing and discussing texts which present issues and relationships between groups and between the individual and society in different historical periods and cultures;
- learning about the social, historical, political and cultural contexts which shape and influence the texts people read and view;
- developing pupils' ability to put their point of view, question, argue and discuss, adapting what they say to their audience and the effect they wish to achieve;
- evaluating critically what they hear, read and view, with attention to explicit and implied meanings, bias and objectivity, and fact and opinion;
- becoming competent users of spoken and written standard English to enable pupils to participate fully in the wider world beyond school, in public life, and in decision-making. (ibid., p. 9)

It is interesting to reflect on the state of the subject in schools, comparing its formulation in the National Curriculum to its initial shape in the wake of the Cox Report (Cox, 1989). Initial curricular conceptions were very literature based, much in line with teachers' thinking in the late 1980s about the core of their subject. The present shape divides the curriculum into 'knowledge, skills and understanding' on the one hand, and 'breadth of study' on the other. The first general change to note is that the English curriculum has moved away from a narrow literature base to one which embraces a range of genres: non-fiction, including argument, has a more secure place than in the late 1980s. Secondly, and not unrelated, the basis of the English curriculum is broader and more language oriented. There is more recognition of the diversity of the language in its spoken and written forms and – crucially – more openness to diversity within culture. The hope is that teachers will interpret the curriculum to mean that 'Englishness' is about diversity and tolerance rather than a more narrowly conceived partisan notion in which 'heritage' and an unrelenting 'standard English' is foisted upon the population. One heartening move forward is the much higher profile afforded to argument in the curriculum, both orally and in writing. In earlier conceptions of the English curriculum, this component was occluded by narrative – the dominant discoursal paradigm of the 1980s.

The broadening and balancing out of the English curriculum is accompanied, however, by some unresolved problems and several anachronisms. There is still reference to 'non-chronological writing' (ibid., e.g. p. 26) as though fiction could be cast as 'chronological' and all other writing as 'non-chronological'. This unhelpful categorization is the subject of a critique in Gibson and Andrews (1993). Despite the references to 'viewing' in the general statements on how English will impact on pupils' learning across the curriculum, there is no statutory requirement for its teaching in the curriculum. The English curriculum, therefore, remains print based in its conception. Speaking and listening are conjoined in one 'programme of study' whereas reading and writing have separate ones. It is clear that either the writers of the curriculum do not see the reciprocity of reading and writing, or they conceive of speaking and listening's reciprocity as warranting less curricular space than that afforded to reading and writing. Furthermore, the emphasis on 'phonemic awareness and phonic knowledge' is highlighted, particularly for children aged 5–11, as a result of pressure during the 1990s to 'toughen up' the teaching of literacy (see the discussions elsewhere in this book, especially in Chapters 3 and 4).

Despite modest advances – and it will probably be generally acknow-ledged that this is a more balanced, more precise and more open curriculum than the 1990 or 1995 versions – there remains the concern that the slow, lumbering process of curricular reform is falling behind changes in the actual experience of language and communication in society. Such a perception is not merely the observation of a clichéd reaction to the pace of change. Rather, it is the result of a growing awareness that schooling and curriculum are losing touch with the real contexts in which learning takes place. The drivers behind the changing landscape for learning include an increasing access for families to multimedia and the Internet in the home; the gradual disappearance of the idea of 'education' as being a separate bolt-on dimension for cultural institutions, but rather it becoming a central part of their identity and function; a dissatisfaction among parents and children with conventional teaching techniques designed to gain maximum results for the school in its fight to rise up the league tables of performance; and changing literacies (e.g. the creation of websites by children and young people) that are not recognized within the formal curriculum. In pragmatic terms, England and Wales still lag behind other countries in the world in terms of their understanding of the relationships between 'viewing' and literacy; in terms of the scope for collaboration across the curriculum in the secondary years; in terms of their over-emphasis on the grapho-phonemic levels in the learning of reading and writing; and in their slowness in recognizing the value of real-world experiences to inspire and inform literacy development. The development of information and communication technologies – including, as I write, the inclusion of digital short and feature-length films online through broadband technology is only a part of the changing social patterns and contexts for literacy development.

Indeed, Cliff Hodges *et al.* (2000) feel that the radical thinking that has been going on in the subject in the 1990s has failed to have much impression on policy and on the revision of the National Curriculum in England for 2000. They see it as imperative that researchers and thinkers, English teachers and policy-makers get together – if necessary on a worldwide basis – to ensure that future revisions of the curriculum in different countries are informed by a coherent and contemporary sense of what constitutes the subject.

The range of English

It was said at the beginning of this chapter that 'English' as a discipline is fragmenting and in danger of falling apart altogether. The range of areas of research within the discipline may reinforce that notion. Protherough, in his first index for the academic/professional flagship journal of the National Association for the Teaching of English (Protherough, 1992), sets out the following headings – among others – in his subject index. I quote only some of those listed under A to C to indicate the range:

Advanced level – assessment
Advanced level – courses
Advanced level – teaching
Africa
Alphabet
America
Argument
Asia
Assessment
Bernstein
Bilingualism
Bullock Report
Certificate of Secondary Education[3]
Carnival
Children's literature
Class
Classroom research
Cloze
Comics
Communication
Comprehension
Continuity
Creativity
Critical theory
Culture
Curriculum

International perspectives

The subtitle of Peel *et al.*'s (2000) book, *Questions of English*, gives an indication of its range of reference: 'ethics, aesthetics, rhetoric and the formation of the subject in England, Australia and the United States.' The book is based on historical analysis and recent research and attempts to compare new insights on curriculum development in the three countries. There are sections on each country and on the key issues in them for English teachers. These are characterized as questions of history, theory and curriculum for England; questions of pedagogy for Australia; and questions of practice and individual expression for the United States – though, clearly, the issues are common to all three countries.

In his introduction, Peel cites the work of Davies (1996), who 'argues that the inability to make a clear distinction between literacy and the subject English, between the subject name and the language name resulted in a National Curriculum [in England] that "fudges the distinction between specialist English and general literacy . . . [and] renders hopeless all attempts at coherence in the subject's structure"' (2000: 1). This is an important distinction, particularly as current governments, driven by economic competitiveness, seem to have a concern about literacy rather than English. It is a real concern when we consider the figures on those attaining functional literacy in Britain compared to those in other OECD countries, for example (see Werquin *et al.*, 2000). He also cites the work of Goodwyn and Fox (1993) on models of English, mentioned earlier in this chapter, pointing out that teachers in England placed a cultural criticism model much higher than did their colleagues in the USA, as if English was seen as a subversive subject – one that provided a critique of culture in all its forms (including schooling and the curriculum!).

This critical dimension is not confined to England, however. In their survey of English teachers' attitudes and beliefs, Peel *et al.* (2000) found that if there was one quality that English curricula and practices shared worldwide, it was the propensity to *ask questions*. Furthermore, if the subject was *about* anything, it was about self-questioning and the exploration of the notion of 'self'. The latter point would seem to reinforce the general finding of Goodwyn's research – that even into the late 1990s, teachers still believed the core business of English was 'personal growth' rather than, say, textual exploration, rhetoric, education in the basic skills or cultural criticism. As Reid (forthcoming) suggests, the forefather of English as a subject may well be Wordsworth rather than Arnold. At core, the subject seems to be about self and the exploration of notions of self.

Implications for practice

The emergence of English as a school and university subject and discipline, and the different models of English that teachers adopt to underpin their teaching, both have implications for practice. The curriculum subject is derived in large part from the university discipline which has imparted a strong literary character on the subject. The literary influence is likely to continue, with the majority of graduates coming into teaching having a degree (or the majority of elements in it) in literature. But if, in a decade which is likely to see teachers in short supply and big demand, graduates in other related subjects can be persuaded to apply for primary and secondary teacher training programmes, the character of the subject could gradually change. Of the different models that have been set out in the present chapter, no single model satisfactorily catches the totality of English. A new, unifying model of English will have to embrace literary study; digital text theory; the skills and capabilities associated with learning to speak, listen, read and write; still and moving images and their relation to verbal codes; multilingualism; and the range of topics indicated in the list above.

The immediate implications for teachers of the subject in England and Wales are that the National Curriculum, as statutorily framed, is only the minimum requirement for teaching and learning. Pragmatically, it can be used as a checklist to make sure the curriculum has been properly covered; or as a proto-planning document, a starting point for learning design. But it cannot serve as a template for a rich and varied programme for English, nor can it obviate the need for creative, imaginative thinking about language and its application. In other countries, national standards frameworks or equivalents to national curricula (whether statutory or optional) place different emphases on aspects of the English curriculum, and thus different demands on teachers and pupils.

Notes

1   The relationship between letters and sounds in the formation of words in English.
2   The Technical and Vocational Education Initiative, promoted by the Training Agency in the 1980s to enhance the vocational dimension of the curriculum and make it more suitable for the world of work.
3   Established in the late 1970s to serve the needs of children who would benefit from a coursework/portfolio approach to assessment in English at 16; it demised in the mid-1980s with the advent of the General Certificate in Secondary Education which combined the market for the General Certificate in Education with that of CSE to form a single examination at 16 in England and Wales.

Chapter 2

Speaking and Listening

The recent history of speaking and listening in the English curriculum is important to chart, with key points in its development being in the mid-1970s and the mid-1980s. In the 1960s, the growing disaffection in England for public examinations in English at 15 or 16, coupled with a sense that the traditional Ordinary level examination did not cater for as many as 80 per cent of the population, gave rise to a new examination, the Certificate in Secondary Education. This examination was radical at the time in that it based much of its assessment on coursework or portfolios of work completed during the course of the two years running up to school-leaving age. Furthermore, it incorporated a spoken element into the assessment. 'CSE orals' usually involved a talk by the student, addressed to the teacher/examiner in 'examination conditions' and followed by a question-and-answer session. It was formal and artificial, but an important step forward in establishing speaking and listening in the assessed curriculum.

Another landmark was 1986, when the General Certificate in Secondary Education replaced the two-tier system of the previous years. The GCSE examination placed – at least in its early years – great emphasis on coursework and instituted spoken English as an essential part of English as a whole. Much effort was expended on moderating spoken performance by students in order to ensure fair and consistent assessment of their work; but perhaps most significant was a diversification of the forms in which speech was explored and examined. Rather than just a stilted 'talk' to the teacher, GCSE offered a range of speech genres including group discussion, interview, formal debate and talks to groups of peers or other audiences. There was heightened awareness of audience and context to complement and inform the increased range in discourse types. Fifteen to twenty years on, the situation remains much the same. This aspect of the English curriculum has struggled to establish itself. One example of this struggle has been the continued (and understandable) yoking together of speaking and listening as reciprocal entities, as in this book, with the resultant underplaying of listening – largely because it is less easily assessable than the other three core components of the subject: speaking, reading and writing.

Issues that have arisen in the last twenty to thirty years as a result of the rise in significance of spoken English include the debate about spoken standard English, the role of dialect and accent, the links between spoken and written English and the place of storytelling in primary and secondary education.

The place of speaking and listening in the English curriculum

Anderson and Hilton (1997) concur that in comparison 'with reading and writing, our understanding of talk is still in its infancy' (p. 12). They cite not only the emergence of speaking and listening in the curriculum, but a major project in England and Wales in the late 1980s and early 1990s, the National Oracy Project, as taking forward practice and awareness about oracy. Nevertheless, their article points out that despite ground-breaking research and practice, the various developments and initiatives had 'yet to yield a conceptual apparatus which teachers [could] incorporate into useful models for teaching and learning' (p. 13). This lack of conceptual backbone is seen as the result of a decade (the 1990s) driven by assessment rather than by learning development, and one which threw up half-baked and often misleading schemes for assessing children's progress in speaking and listening (as well as other areas of the English curriculum). As Anderson and Hilton put it:

> If we are to develop a rich and empowering curriculum with regard to spoken language in the primary school then privileging issues of assessment is putting the cart before the horse. A comprehensive and developed framework which takes account of research on how language works in society and how children acquire, use and embellish it is the place to begin. (1997: 15)

They conclude that a conceptual framework for speaking and listening in the primary classroom 'would take account of two powerful traject-ories' (p. 21). These are 'the enculturated *development of personhood,* which starts with *familial discourses* and is quickly adapted and transformed by the *discourses of the popular media.* The second is the *academic and moral discourses of school* with its framing of knowledge within a national, intellectual and educational culture' (pp. 21–2). In other words, Anderson and Hilton argue for a closer connection between the language of home, media and street on the one hand, and that of school on the other, feeling that the latter is impoverished without consideration and influence of the former.

Spoken standard English

Bernstein (1971) established a strong connection between speech and the social structures in which learners of any age acquired language: 'the speech form is taken as a consequence of the form of the social relation or, put more generally, is a quality of the social structure' (p. 172). But he qualifies this general principle: 'Because the speech form is initially a function of a given social arrangement, it does not mean that the speech form does not in turn modify or even change that social structure' (ibid.). Nevertheless, social shaping is the primary determinant of speech development, and of the factors affecting home, school, work and the peer group – the main communities in which speech is learnt – Bernstein identifies class as the 'most formative influence' (ibid., p. 172). In terms of speech patterning, he argues that 'forms of socialization orient the child towards speech codes which control access to relatively context-tied or relatively context-independent meanings' and goes on to suggest that 'elaborated codes orient their users towards universalistic [context-independent] meanings, whereas restricted codes orient, sensitize, their users to particularistic [context-dependent] meanings' (idem). While it is not possible in the confines of this book to give a full account of Bernstein's position, it is possible to say that his distinction between 'elaborated' and 'restricted' codes has had a considerable impact on thinking about the use of speech in the primary and secondary school, and in particular on the home–school relationship. Essentially, the differences posited by Bernstein are set out in the following table:

Elaborated code	Restricted code
Universalistic	Particularistic
Context-independent	Context-dependent
Limited access by some classes	
Less tied to given or local social structures	More tied to given or local social structures
An individual has more access to the grounds of his/her socialization, and so can enter into a reflexive relationship with it	An individual has less access to the grounds of his/her socialization, and so cannot enter into a reflexive relationship with it
Articulated symbols	Condensed symbols
Rationality	Metaphor
	Range of syntactic alternatives (sentence structures) is likely to be reduced
	Lexis (vocabulary) drawn from a narrower range
Difference lies at the basis of the social relationship, and is made verbally active	Consensus: intent of the other person can be taken for granted, because of shared social assumptions
Individualization: realized through elaborated speech variants	Speech cannot be understood apart from the context, and context cannot be read by those who are not party to it
Concern with the form and structure of communication	Less need to raise meanings to the level of explicitness or elaboration; less need to make clear the logical structure of the communication

Bernstein (1971) is at pains to point out that 'because the code is restricted it does not mean that speakers at no time will not use elaborated speech variants, only that such use will be infrequent in the socialization of the child in his family'. But one of the key aspects of his research as far as schooling is concerned is the potential mismatch between the elaborated code of schools and the restricted code of some children who attend them. A crucial passage is:

> Let it be said . . . that a restricted code gives access to a vast potential
> of meanings, of delicacy, subtlety and diversity of cultural forms,
> to a unique aesthetic the basis of which in condensed symbols may

influence the form of the imagining. Yet, in complex industrialized societies its differently-focused experience may be disvalued and humiliated within schools, or seen, at best, to be irrelevant to the educational endeavour. For the schools are predicated upon an elaborated code and its system of social relationships. Although an elaborated code does not entail any specific value system, the value system of the middle class penetrates the texture of the very learning context itself. (Bernstein, 1972: 109)

Bernstein's position is usually placed in opposition to that of Labov's, as expressed in 'The logic of nonstandard English' (1972), but inevitably the opposition is over-simplified to make a clear contrast. Labov's essay takes as its starting point the verbal deficit theory. In fact, Labov defines his position in opposition to an earlier work of Bernstein's in which Bernstein proposes that 'much of lower-class language consists of a kind of incidental "emotional" accompaniment to action here and now' (p. 118). Labov argues that Operation Headstart and other intervention programmes have been largely based on the deficit theory which itself is a combination of prejudices and experiments designed to confirm those prejudices. Through careful analysis of interviews and focus group sessions with young black Americans, Labov debunks the deficit theory, proving that these young people have as sophisticated and complex language at hand as middle-class 'elaborated' code speakers. Labov prefers to refer to Bernstein's formulation as an elaborated style rather than as a mode, seeing it as just one of the possible styles that a school might employ to educate its pupils. Furthermore, Labov sees the nonstandard as just as able to deal with complexity as the standard dialects of the language:

> It is often said that the nonstandard vernacular is not suited for dealing with abstract or hypothetical questions, but in fact speakers from the NNE [nonstandard Negro English] community take great delight in exercising their wit and logic on the most improbable and problematical matters. (1972: 204)

Labov finds, in general, six flawed propositions behind the verbal deficit theories. These are:

- the lower-class child's verbal response to a formal and threatening situation is used to demonstrate his lack of verbal capacity, or verbal deficit;

- this verbal deficit is declared to be a major cause of the lower-class child's poor performance in school;
- since middle-class children do better in school, middle-class speech habits are seen to be necessary for learning;
- class and ethnic differences in grammatical form are equated with differences in the capacity for logical analysis;
- teaching the child to mimic certain formal speech patterns used by middle-class teachers is seen as teaching him to think logically;
- children who learn these formal speech patterns are then said to be thinking logically and it is predicted that they will do much better in reading and arithmetic in the years to follow. (1972: 207)

While the Bernstein/Labov debate of the late 1960s and early 1970s took place over a generation ago, there are still inequalities in educational performance, issues of class differentiation and debates on the place of standard and nonstandard speech forms in relation to education and schooling. It could be said, with hindsight, that we now know more about the difference between written standard English (generally accepted then, as now, as tenable and worth fighting for) and spoken standard English, which is now seen as one of a number of dialects possible outside and inside schools; and that this distinction is central to making sense of the debate. It is now more generally accepted in research that the language children bring to school is the language in which they should be educated; at the same time, that learning different codes is beneficial to each student because it enables him/her to operate in a number of different communities; and that spoken development is as important as written development. Policy and practice do not always reflect such an open-minded approach.

Whitehead (1993), for instance, points out that children come to school at age four, five or six already well on the way to developing capability in a range of spoken and written forms; and those children who are exposed to more than one language or dialect in their early childhood often show a well-developed linguistic and metalinguistic awareness. Furthermore, language is always changing as it is, in part, a reflection of the society in which it forms part of the fabric. It follows that attempts to impose a 'spoken standard English' are fraught with tensions of different kinds. Engel and Whitehead (1996) develop the argument further. They suggest that the supposed 'spoken standard' version changes too, but possibly at a slower rate than the vernacular:

> The very term 'standard' implies a stability and conservatism born of prestige and very often linked to a close relationship between its spoken and written manifestations. It is characterised by codification (such as prescriptive grammar books, linguistic etiquette, language academies) and the elaboration of function (use for education, administration, and so forth). (p. 37)

It is important to recognize that spoken standard English is a dialect rather than a language or an accent. It is possible to speak standard English – which is characterized by its grammar and vocabulary – with any kind of accent. It is also generally accepted that standard English, in both its written and spoken versions, 'can indeed open up a wider world of experience, culture and opportunity to children' (Engel and Whitehead, 1996: 38), and that bilingualism or multilingualism are now recognized as assets rather than complications in schooling. There is increasing evidence, however, that in the UK children who are bilingual or multilingual are in danger of losing their native or first language (if it is other than English) unless they get support through home and/or community to use that or those languages. In the case of speakers of other British dialects too, the sense of identity can be threatened by an over-emphasis on spoken standard English. Spoken standard English, then, can oppress as well as liberate. Whitehead (1993) concludes that 'we have a duty of scholarship and care to inform families and communities, legislators and administrators' (p. 45) that young children are linguistically competent; that young bilinguals are even more advantaged in their linguistic potential; that standard forms of languages are evolving dialects which reflect commercial, religious, social and political power; that nonstandard dialects are also evolving and have their own roles in the lives of their speakers; and that monolingual speakers are the linguistic minorities of the world who are disadvantaged.

Speaking and listening at home and at school

One of the most significant studies of the last thirty years or so has been Gordon Wells's longitudinal research into the language development of a group of children from pre-school through the primary years, examining the environmental and contextual factors. The Bristol University study, 'Language at Home and at School', ran from 1969 to 1984 under Wells's direction and is written up in a number of books (e.g. Wells, 1981, 1985a, 1985b, 1987; Wells and Nicholls, 1985). There were a number of insights that emerged during and after the research that have shed light on the field of language development in speaking and listening.

The first of these is that there were 'substantial differences between children in their rate of language development' (Wells, 1985a: viii–ix). While this was not unexpected, there was a 'generally rather low level of correlation . . . between rate of language development and class of family background' (p. ix). These results led Wells and his team to have 'grave reservations about any simple statements of relationship between pre-school oral language development, class and subsequent attainment' (ibid.). Indeed, rather than see such a connection, Wells suggests that a more important factor is the quality of the child's conversational experience:

> The key to the enigma of where language comes from, I suggest, is to be found in interaction: interaction between learners who are predisposed to make sense of their experience, including their experience of linguistic communication, and a community of more mature language users who provide the evidence on which the learners construct their representation of the language system. Differences in rate of learning can be explained, at least in part, in terms of the quality of this evidence and of the manner in which it is provided. In this second sense also, therefore, interaction provides the key. In the form of conversation, linguistic interaction is both the means and the goal for language learning. (Ibid.)

Other additions to the research literature are the importance of 'knowledge of literacy' as a predictor of educational attainment at age seven (by comparison, differences of oral language ability were found to be much less significant); the suggestion that the language of the classroom in the early years could be as diverse and engaging as the language most children experience at home; and confirmation of the importance of storytelling, not only in the early years but throughout education. The implications for teachers are clear in the light of Wells's research: teachers, he argues, should be 'much more cautious about accepting the theories of linguists and psychologists as a basis for classroom practice in the teaching of reading and writing' and – particularly pertinent to the present book – although research on language can provide insights about the nature of language itself, 'the theories that will be most helpful for teachers are those that they construct for themselves' (p. xi). Finally, to take the emphasis on language itself, Wells suggests that life will be more challenging and rewarding for teachers and children alike 'when learning is seen as a collaborative activity in which all participants are recognized to be actively and responsibly engaged in the making of meaning' (ibid.).

Storytelling

Storytelling has been a significant part of the spoken English curriculum in primary – and, to an extent, secondary – education since the early 1980s. I described the value of a secondary curriculum based on storytelling in an account of work in the East End of London (Andrews, 1981) in which a local storyteller made regular visits to a class of 13/14-year-olds, transforming their sense of the power of narrative and providing a basis from which they could experiment with their own exploration of the differences between spoken and written stories. The work on storytelling in the 1980s was supported by theories of the power and ubiquity of narrative in human discourse, characterized by publications like Rosen (1985) and Fisher (1987). Essentially, publications like these built up narrative to be a 'human paradigm' and ever-present determinant of the way we think and organize our lives rather than just one of a number of types of discourse in human interaction. At its best, this movement promoted storytelling and a renewed interest in the construction of written narratives in all their different forms; at worst, it erected narrative into an orthodoxy, reducing the value and status of the other forms of discourse like lyric expression, argumentation and dialogue.

Boyle (1998), for example, cites some of the published articles and books that have reflected and partly brought about the ascendency of narrative and story. These include Barbara Hardy's famous statement 'narrative is a primary act of mind, transferred from life to art', Meek (1977), Wells (1987) and Fox (1993). Boyle gives an account of an ethnographic research study in which story was used as the basis of cross-curricular approaches to cognitive development. While accounting for the success of the curricular experiment, Boyle also proposes that it was the power of the storytelling itself which provided the motivation and engagement for a range of learning outcomes for the five-year-old children involved.

Withington (1996) looks in particular at a six-year-old storyteller, Navdeep, and at how his stories bridge two cultures. First, she explores some of the background to the power and ubiquity of stories in children's lives, quoting Fox's (1993) 'we should expect to find in their invented stories all their theories about the world' (1996: 29–30). She finds, in the told stories of this six-year-old, that he 'makes sense' of his Sikh heritage by incorporating elements of Eastern and Western culture into his stories, fusing them in acts of the imagination. Collins (1996) sets out what she sees as the key ingredients of storytelling, following a study in which she surveyed fifty storytellers at work in Britain at the time. These include children's enthusiasm for stories *told* by tellers and the clear benefits for those children who are struggling with school. Another finding was that children have a wholehearted commitment to the 'truth' of stories. We need to be reminded here that such a commitment is a stage in cognitive development preceding that which understands that encyclopedias and 'non-fiction' sources contain the truth; only to be superseded, in turn, by a view that is sceptical about the relativity of such truths.[1] As adults, we have moved through these stages (some of us not always as far as the third stage!) but perhaps we also incorporate each of the stages we have passed through in our present sensibility: otherwise we would not be able to suspend disbelief and immerse ourselves in the world of a play or novel.

Collins points out the value in accepting a number of possible worlds:

> For children who are so afraid of making a mistake that they hardly ever begin anything, and frequently destroy their work because they cannot achieve the perfection they have prescribed for themselves, the opportunity to explore the notion of relative truth, and in particular the idea that there is more than one right answer to many questions – and even more questions to which the right answer can never be known, but only guessed at – the experience of exploring different versions of truth through creation stories and myths is a helpful, constructive and enlightening one. (1996: 42)

An analogy is proposed between 'the skills of the preliterate child, of whatever age and ability, and the working methods used by the expert storyteller, of whatever time or culture' (p. 43). This interesting analogy opens up the possibility of recognizing oral abilities for what they are:

not sub-literate activities, or at best precursors to literacy, but 'oracy' skills in their own right that need more recognition than they receive in the literacy-driven school curriculum.

In a chapter called 'The Irrepressible Genre', Harold Rosen (1988) notes that research into narrative and particularly storytelling has tended to fall into two camps: on the one hand, the 'text only' work of Rumelhart (1975) and others who have tended to focus on 'story grammars'; and, on the other hand, studies of narrative in performance. The distinction echoes that of 'langue' and 'parole' in Saussurian linguistics, with emphases on system and realization in the world respectively. Rosen's 'negative stock-taking' (1988: 15) suggests that there is relatively little on spontaneous, naturally occurring narrative; even less on oral narrative as argument; little on oral narrative in modern, urban, industrialized societies; hazy conceptions of bilingual narrative; and the need for an educational theory of narrative. He attacks Bruner (1986) for dwelling on written, achieved, literary narrative in the exposition of narrative in *Actual Minds, Possible Worlds*, as opposed to exploring oral narratives in more depth.

What Smith (1981), Rosen and others take for granted is that narrative (the overarching mode of discourse) and storytelling or anecdote (particular spoken text types or 'genres'[2]) can appear not only as a distinct form in its own right but is often interwoven with other modes of discourse to create hybrid forms. There has been a good deal of work on narrative and its relation to argument (see Andrews, 1989), which is discussed in more detail in Chapter 3 of this book. The important point to note in this particular chapter on storytelling is that story itself can embrace a range of different styles, from the dialogic to the monologic, from folk tale to anecdote, or from simple to elaborate. I found that in a year nine English class I taught in the East End of London, the pupils' told stories were on the whole shorter, more focused on plot and more dramatic than the written versions, which concentrated on the build-up of character and setting and which used a larger range of vocabulary. Analysis of the transcripts of the told stories alongside the written stories revealed not only broad-brush differences such as these, but a different grammar at work. Told stories were like speech, following a grammar that was not sentence bound, which repeated itself in rhythmic style and which drew on an informal diction; written stories were sentence bound (often using compound and complex sentence structure), varied in rhythmic style and elaborate.

Such distinctions between speech and writing can be misleading, however. It is probably erroneous to suggest that speech always precedes writing, that speech is a more direct and briefer mode of expression, that speech is always more dialogic than writing, and so on. While general truths are evident – for example, that children learn to speak before they learn to write, so that, as Vygotsky has put it, writing is a 'second order symbolic system' – it needs to be acknowledged that such symbolic systems as writing can provide a basis and model for certain kinds of speech.

Classroom talk

One of the most significant pieces of research in speaking and listening in classrooms is Barnes, Britton and Rosen's *Language, the Learner and the School* (1969).[3] It was significant in its time because classroom talk had received little formal attention up to that point; and it is significant now not only because of its historical importance to the development of English, but also because it remains a fresh and challenging look at classroom discourse and how learning takes place through speaking and listening.

In the third edition (1986) the authors reflect on the research they originally undertook in the late 1960s. Their first concern is 'to show how classroom talk can make for good learning' (p. 7). Positioning themselves firmly against a transmission model of teaching, they see the dialogue between a teacher and his/her class, and between students in the class, as the central foundation on which learning is built: it emerges from the principles of 'conversation' and what teachers already know about such discourse. The book consists of three separate papers – one by each of the authors – the first two arising from the work of a group of practising teachers: the first paper looks at classroom talk (Barnes), the second at the relationship of language to learning (Britton) and the third (Rosen/Torbe) at whole school language policies, both before and in the wake of the influential Bullock Report (1975).

Barnes's study looked at the kinds of questions asked by teachers in classrooms of 11- and 12-year-olds, and at the kinds of responses from students; but also at questions asked by students and how teachers responded to them. Questions were divided into the following categories: factual (or 'what'? questions), reasoning (how? and why?), open questions not calling for reasoning and social questions concerned with the management of the class. Barnes found that there were fewer factual questions asked in the five English classes he examined than in similar classes in Maths, History or RE; that reasoning questions were also low in comparison to these subjects (except History); and that social questions had a high incidence. Perhaps most interestingly, open questions (i.e. questions to which 'a number of different answers would be acceptable') had the highest proportionate incidence in English, though some of these might be 'pseudo-questions' which purport to be open but through which the teacher is seeking a specific answer (one that is in his or her head). In the particular classrooms in which the research was undertaken, the open questions in English 'were largely ones requiring the pupils to find likenesses between two poems; the teacher accepted a wide range of replies relating either to form or to meaning' (p. 22). If we consider learning to be a transformation on the part of the learner in relation to the recoding that is required in a classroom, it is heartening to think that in this particular examination of classroom discourse, nearly half the questions were found to be 'open', allowing space for the students to reformulate knowledge on their own terms – or in terms of what they bring to the lessons.

Much of what actually happens in English lessons, both at primary and secondary level, could be described as 'demonstrated thought'; that is to say, the teacher uses the students to provide answers to preconceived – apparently open but often more closed – questions. These answers provide the beads on a string that the teacher him- or herself is threading. Understanding a particular process or idea means 'seeing' the unity of the stringed beads to which the students have contributed. They are then usually asked to re-present the string in some other form or format (e.g. essay, notes, story, front page of a newspaper or report). The fallacy in this very common approach is that it is assumed, always tacitly, that the construction that is made in the air, in words, will somehow permeate into the minds of the students.

What was – and is – so striking about Barnes's research is that it demonstrated that active engagement with ideas and processes in the classroom *by students* is a much more effective way of ensuring engagement and, subsequently, understanding – not to mention the pleasure derived from engagement. In an important passage (p. 58), Barnes notes:

> It is when the pupil is required to use language to grapple with new experience or to order old experience in a new way that he is most likely to find it necessary to use language differently . . . it is

the first step towards new patterns of thinking and feeling, new ways of representing reality to himself [sic]. It is not enough for pupils to imitate the forms of teachers' language as if they were models to be copied; it is only when they 'try it out' in reciprocal exchanges . . . that they are able to find new functions for language in thinking and feeling. This would suggest that the low level of pupil participation in these lessons, if they are . . . typical of secondary lessons, is a matter of some educational urgency.

Barnes's essay acted as a starting point for Mitchell's study of the nature and role of questioning in school subjects across the curriculum (Mitchell, 1993b). She points out that Barnes's study is largely based on the categorization of questions by teachers. It does not look, for instance, at sequences of questions and how they weave a logical or quasi-logical thread in the air; nor does it look at students' questions in much depth. (Barnes would probably say this is because, in the classrooms studied in the 1960s, students' questions were not often answered by teachers as if they were genuine questions about knowledge.) Mitchell's own work, in looking at questioning in Politics, History, English and other subjects at a fairly advanced level (16- to 18-year-old classes), concluded that questions were powerful tools in the interaction of classrooms which were not always used to the benefit of learning. She thus reaches a similar conclusion to Barnes, but for different reasons.

Britton's essay in *Language, the Learner and the School* develops his thinking about 'expressive' language – in this case, speech – and its importance to learning in the classroom. In the Britton model, as it came to be known, expressive speech or writing was close to everyday language, full of circumstance, feeling, thought and the mesh of experience. It separated into 'poetic' on the one hand and 'transactional' on the other. Poetic speech or writing tended to be aware of itself and manifested itself in art forms; transactional language got the world's work done. The latter type was a much less self-aware use of language, and more transparent.

Echoing Barnes, Britton writes:

A recognition that talking can be a means of learning; that its effectiveness as such a means relies on a relationship of mutual trust between those taking part in the talk; and that the onus for establishing that relationship in the classroom lies first with the teacher – all this clearly assumes an interactive view of learning;

and this in turn has important implications for our view of the curriculum. (1969: 127)

There is a recognition here that genuine discussion will be exploratory and expressive and will, through the space afforded it by the teacher and the skilful engagement or negotiation with it by the teacher, lead toward the reshaping of knowledge that we look to in our students.

Gender issues

Gender issues manifest themselves in all aspects of language education. Swann's book, *Girls, Boys and Language* (1992), addresses questions of language use, girls' and boys' talk in the classroom, questions of reading choices and other related matters all within a framework of bringing about more equality for girls and boys in education. Delamont (1990) argues that school organization, lesson organization, lesson content, informal conversations between pupils and teachers, and letting pupils' stereotyping of activities go unchallenged are the five main ways in which gender distinctions are maintained in schools.

Swann reviews some of the research (e.g. Halpern, 1986) that suggests that biology and linguistic destiny are not necessarily clearly related. It is wrong, therefore, to assume that girls have more 'linguistic ability' and less 'spatial ability' than boys, and Swann argues that a more balanced approach would not suggest that biological pre-determination is irrelevant, but would set it alongside 'the range of differences between girls' and boys' behaviour, many of which are culturally specific' (pp. 10–11). The social dimension is particularly important in a book devoted to research on language education, as language is assumed to be socially embedded. In the opening chapter, Swann explores the similarities and differences in language use by girls and boys, for instance the research that suggests male speakers tend to interrupt more than female speakers; they make 'direct' requests rather than 'indirect' ones; female speakers tend to give more conversational support and indicate tentativeness in their speech more than male speakers. She also addresses the reinforcement of gender stereotypes through language that occurs in everyday speech, both by male and female speakers and about them. The implications for the classroom are clear:

> Gender differences in language will be maintained or challenged
> in the classroom, as in other contexts. Teachers need to decide how

to respond to girls' and boys' language: to what extent and how girls and boys should be encouraged to adopt different ways of speaking and how gender differences in language should be taken into account in teaching and learning. Knowledge of gender differences can also inform work on language awareness. (p. 47)

As far as the classroom goes, Swann cites considerable evidence that girls' and boys' language behaviour differs in the classroom, with boys dominating the verbal space, especially in subjects which are conventionally the 'territory' of boys, like the sciences, design and technology and computing. An important implication for classrooms is that teachers must be sensitive to the different ways in which boys and girls might use language, and the different learning styles associated with those different modes of discourse.

The metaphorical nature of everyday talk

Metaphor is one of the least well-understood elements in speech and writing and yet one of the most pervasive elements in the fabric of language use. All too often it is 'taught' in English as merely the defining characteristic of poetry, and along with simile is beaten to death in this small corner of the language curriculum. Some teachers tend to choose to 'do' poetry simply in order to identify the metaphors and similes therein – the difference between metaphor and simile being presented as to do with the omission (metaphor) or inclusion (simile) of 'like' or 'as' before the figurative analogy. In discussing the complexity and ubiquity of metaphor in language in this section, I will draw on the work of Lakoff and Johnson (1980), Ashton (1994, 1997), Goddard (1996) and Cameron and Low (1999).

Although metaphor has been the subject of study in linguistics, literature and rhetoric for centuries, the recent revival of interest can be traced back to Lakoff and Johnson's *Metaphors We Live By* (1980). This book, in discussing a number of examples of deeply embedded metaphors in the language of everyday life, charted how metaphors both reflected and informed the way we look at the world.

Take the concept of argument, for example – an important element in the make-up of English at primary and secondary school levels, and also an important mode of discourse in everyday life, in selling and marketing and in the operation of democracies (e.g. through law, parliament and in conflict resolution). Argument is conventionally conceived of in terms of metaphors of war, battle and construction. Arguments are 'fought' and others' arguments 'shot down' or 'destroyed'. The grounds on which argument is played out are 'won' or 'lost'; claims are defended and attacked. Using a different metaphor, arguments are 'built' or 'constructed' stage by stage, with 'foundations', 'structures' and 'reinforcements'; there is even the sense of elaboration or embellishment. Such a constructive and destructive conception of the practice not only informs the understanding of the term 'argument'; it probably also determines the nature of progression in an argument itself. Contrast such conceptions with argument as a dance or as a journey.

Drawing on Black (1971), Ashton (1997) recites three theories of metaphor: as using comparison, substitution and interaction. These three are clearly interrelated, all depending on the bringing together of two different concepts to illuminate one or both. But the recitation of the functions and operations of metaphor does not do justice to the complexity of metaphor as described by classical rhetoricians. Soskice (1989) quotes Aristotle:

> by far the most important is to be good at metaphor. For this is the only one that cannot be learnt from anyone else, and it is a sign of natural genius, as to be good at metaphor is to perceive resemblances. (p. 9)

As Ashton (1997) notes, the 'power of metaphor to enable the reader to share the excitement of the experience with the writer is impressive' (p. 198). In that excitement is a mesh of thought, feeling, perception and values, derived from the particular choice of the metaphor. It cannot, argues Ashton, be disentangled from perception as some writers and the general consensus would have it, namely different from the factual or actual in that it embellishes 'reality': 'distinctions between "literal" and "figurative" are nonsensical' (p. 202).

The educational implications of an appreciation of the functions of metaphor are clear: the recognition and exploration of metaphor in everyday life can be both fun and educative, in that structures of feeling and perception can be revealed and discussed. At the same time, encountering metaphor in literature and across the curriculum can be enlightening in that it will help students both to see and to make connections. Pursuing metaphors in fields like chemistry or geography can deepen an understanding of the way a subject is constructed via an appreciation of the kinds of connection that are made within it. As Ashton (1994) says, 'the interpretation of metaphor involves making comparison of what is known with that which it is wished to know even better' (p. 358). In this way, it is not just affective education that will take place; it is a matter of using metaphor to make cognitive leaps too.

In an interesting article on metaphor, Goddard (1996) unpicks some of the informing metaphors by which we understand English as a subject. In particular, she explores the power bases of metaphor in everyday life, revealing that, for instance, in accounts of rape trials, men are often described 'as if they shouldn't be expected to be in control of themselves, with women often blamed as sources of the heat' (p. 9). Metaphors thus have a power base; they reflect hegemony. Like Ashton, Goddard wishes us to see metaphor as part of the warp and weft of language and experience from an early age, rather than as a sophisticated rhetorical device used in poetry.

In a comprehensive review of writing in applied linguistics on metaphor, Cameron and Low (1999) identify two intellectual traditions in approaches to metaphor: the logical positivist and the constructivist. Again, as we have seen in attempting to elucidate the difference between narrative and story, one approach has in mind the exploration and definition of systems; the other is more willing to accept the differences found in everyday discourse. Typically, educationalists tend toward the constructivist approaches as they seem to offer more scope for qualitative exploration of experience; and researchers in language – particularly from the 1970s onwards – have welcomed the emphasis because it gives them unlimited scope for further research and tends to foreground the linguistic as opposed to conceptual nature of speech and writing. A particularly relevant section of the article by Cameron and Low is devoted to metaphor and language development in both speakers of English as a first and second language. They note that recent research has questioned the notion that children acquire an understanding of the function of metaphor quite late in their development, preferring to think that – like argumentation – the ability to use metaphor and to understand its use are evident in early childhood. They do, however, point to the need for more naturalistic studies and imaginative research methods 'to investigate understanding in discourse and interactional contexts of use, particularly with children of school age and above' (p. 84). In summary, the authors point out that their survey reveals that metaphor takes a range of forms, is ubiquitous, has a large number of functions, is crucial to knowledge of and performance in language and is probably crucial to acquiring a language. At the same time, they indicate that there has been insufficient research to date on metaphor in second-language acquisition and very little on teaching control over metaphor.

The quality of listening

In curricular and research terms, much less time and space is devoted to the serious study of listening than to the study of speaking. It is as if speaking is thought to be the active, productive side of the coin, while listening is the passive side. Perhaps the key work of the last thirty years or so is Wilkinson *et al.*'s *The Quality of Listening* (1974), which even then noted a dearth of research into an aspect of the English (and broader) curriculum that was taken for granted. Nevertheless, the research undertaken by Wilkinson and his colleagues was set against a background which already understood that, on the whole, people listen badly. Truisms like 'the longer people listen, the less they are able to learn' are particularly serious when well over half of students' 'communication time' is spent in listening.

Wilkinson *et al.*'s approach is what we might describe now as a 'whole language' approach: they see the development of listening as tied intimately to the development of speaking, reading and writing rather than see the development of listening skills as a mechanistic and separate activity. In other words, the contexts in which listening takes place are crucially important to its development. Wilkinson *et al.* argue, on the basis of their research evidence, that a wider range of spoken texts needs to be made available to pupils so that they listen critically to this range, thus extending their listening repertoire and providing the basis for critical listening.

A useful reference point for categorizing kinds of listening is Brown and Carlesen's Listening Comprehension Test (1953), not so much for its testing qualities as for the categories generated. These are: immediate recall; following directions; recognizing transitions; recognizing word meanings; and lecture comprehension (i.e. the ability to deduce meanings from context, understand the central idea, draw inferences, understand organization and note the degree of relevance). The taxonomy was based on Brown's earlier (1949) distinction between receptive and reflective listening skills. Receptive skills are primarily to do with accuracy in listening, like the ability to keep related details in mind, the ability to observe a single detail, the ability to remember a series of details and the ability to follow oral directions. Reflective skills include the ability to use contextual clues, to recognize organizational elements, to select main ideas as opposed to subordinate ideas and details, the ability to recognize the relationship between main and subordinate ideas, and the ability to draw justifiable inferences.

Little was added in the second half of the twentieth century to shed more light on the processes of listening.

Implications for practice

The struggle (by linguists and educationalists) to establish the distinction between accent and dialect in the minds of policy-makers has been a long one. It seems that the battle has been won, and that curricula are now much more aware of the *social* and *political* nature of distinctions between these and between spoken standard English. There is still confusion – or perhaps a deliberate conflation – between written standard English and spoken standard. They are not the same thing, and operate from different grammars. The situation within England is complicated when one looks to the other countries of the UK, and then to the wider world. 'English' as spoken in the USA, Australia and, say, Papua New Guinea is more than a dialect; it is a language in its own right, with distinctive grammatical and lexical characteristics, let alone pronunciation differences.

Perhaps the lessons to be learned from such diversity, and from other aspects of research into speaking and listening in the curriculum, are as follows:

- Each country and nation will want to determine its exact political position in relation to the English language, whether it is a first, second or third language in the curriculum.
- Distinctions between accent, dialect and 'spoken standard English' need to be reinforced and revisited, with the latter being considered carefully by different cultures in the light of the local and international political needs.
- Classroom talk needs to be celebrated and periodically reviewed, with schools determining the kinds of talk they wish to encourage in lessons. Talking to learn continues to be an important part of the curriculum (across the curriculum as well

as in English). There are implications for classroom management style here, as well as for the way in which computers are deployed in the school and the talk that goes on around them.

- Storytelling, with its foundations in narrative, might be employed more in the secondary curriculum as well as the primary. In the present climate, with increasing pressure on performance against literacy targets, it is important to remember the power of storytelling in the primary curriculum too.
- Metaphor is part of the fabric of everyday talk and much more pervasive in culture than its formal appearance in poetry and poetry teaching. Opportunities to discuss metaphor should be seized, as should opportunities to talk about other aspects of language, like etymology, word construction and variation.
- We need to continue to try to give status and recognition to listening in the curriculum. All too often, the acts of speaking – which are more tangible and apparently more productive and creative – gain precedence over listening.

Notes

1   This book, for example, presents research underpinning attitudes towards teaching and learning English. But it is, of necessity, a *selection* from the research undertaken in the last thirty or so years. That selection determines the nature of the research base. So it is probably not entirely possible to say that the truth of a situation is x, when y is bound by the contingencies of selection.

2   The term 'genre' is a complex one, with a range of meanings. The so-called 'Sydney School' of researchers sees genre as equivalent to a text-type, i.e. a classifiable, identifiable kind of speech or writing; at the other end of the spectrum, sociologically driven notions of genre in North America, in the wake of Miller (1984), have seen genre as a situated cluster of social factors resulting in an identifiable social type of discourse, e.g. the patent. As with the Saussurian distinction mentioned in the text, the former tends to prefer systematic 'text only' approaches and the latter is more sensitive to context and situation.

3   The book has been published in several editions since 1969. In 1971 an expanded edition was published by the same authors, and in 1986 a third edition was issued with Mike Torbe replacing Harold Rosen. Subsequent editions have appeared in the USA.

Chapter 3

Learning to Write

We have seen in earlier chapters that gaining command of reading and writing implies capability in working at the different levels at which language operates, and being able to integrate those levels in the service of some communicative need. It follows that research into learning to write covers a wide range of areas: from research into the grapho-phonemic relationships in English to research into the morphological level, vocabulary acquisition, syntactic structures, writing in paragraphs and other sub-textual units, whole text composition and beyond. In short, the field covers research into spelling, grammar, the writing process, different genres and forms of language and the deployment of language. It is a vast field in which there is a large amount of research. This chapter aims to select key research in the area and to integrate it for application in the classroom.

Composition and transcription

One of the most important distinctions in the field of teaching and learning writing is that between composition and transcription. Smith (1982) made the distinction in order to distinguish between the authorial acts of composing in words on the one hand, and the secretarial business of getting words onto the page or screen in a lucid, accurate manner on the other.

The following table illustrates the relationship:

Composition	Transcription
Getting ideas	Physical effort of writing or typing
Shaping and rearranging ideas	Paragraphs and other sub-units of text
Grammar/style	Punctuation
Selecting words	Spelling
	Capitalization, etc.
	Legibility

The distinction is useful in a number of ways. First, because it separates two aspects of writing that can muddle the writer if conflated, often causing a 'writing block' because the attention is on the surface when it should be on the deeper features of the composition. Second, because in the practice of drafting and redrafting, attention in schools is all too often on the surface features again, rather than on 'deep' redrafting. It is no wonder that pupils often complain about redrafting if they are getting little from it other than surface polishing. Third, because it enables a pedagogic approach to the teaching of writing that is sensitive to the different stages in the act of writing.

Such a distinction does not mean to say that it always has to come into play. There are some occasions for writing when drafting is not appropriate and a distinction between composition and transcription would be unhelpful (e.g. the writing of short notes, the recording of an interview, the quick penning of a personal letter). What is important, however, is that both sides of the act of writing need to be borne in mind: it would not be useful to have a pedagogy of writing that only concentrated on composition or only on transcription. It is also important to note that the authorial and the secretarial are roles rather than different people. As Smith says, 'for most of us, for most of the time, there is no such division of labor; we have to play both roles concurrently' (1982: 20). And lastly, as a caveat, Smith warns that 'composition and transcription can interfere with each other. The more attention you give to one, the more the other is likely to suffer' (p. 21).

A more specific study was carried out by Emig (1971), in a revision of her doctoral dissertation, which examined the composing processes of twelfth-grade writers (15- to 16-year-olds), using a case-study method. Eight twelfth graders of above average and average ability were asked, in four sessions each, to give autobiographies of their writing experiences and to compose aloud three themes in the presence of a tape recorder and the investigator. As Emig describes the study:

Four hypotheses were formulated about their accounts and their writing behaviors:

1. Twelfth-grade writers engage in two modes of composing – reflexive and extensive – characterized by processes of different lengths with different clusterings of components.
2. These differences can be ascertained and characterized through having twelfth-grade writers compose aloud – that is, attempting to externalize their processes of composing.
3. In the composing processes of twelfth-grade writers, an implied or an explicit set of stylistic principles governs the selection and arrangement of components – lexical, syntactic, rhetorical, imagaic.
4. For twelfth-grade writers extensive writing occurs chiefly as a school-sponsored activity; reflexive, as a self-sponsored activity. (1971: 3)

The reflexive mode 'focuses upon the writer's thoughts and feelings concerning his experiences; the chief audience is the writer himself; the domain explored is often the affective; the style is tentative, personal and exploratory' (p. 4). The extensive mode is more audience focused and the domain usually cognitive; the style is 'assured, impersonal and often reportorial' (ibid.).

While Emig's particular taxonomy has been lost in a welter of different taxonomies of written forms and processes (cf. Moffett, 1968; Britton *et al.*, 1975 and more recent curricular categories), what does stand out is her commitment to a humanistic, qualitatively based case-study approach to the investigation of writing.

Writing development

Many of the early objections to the National Curriculum for English in England and Wales were that it was based on a linear model of progression, whereas actual development in English was recursive. In practice, students are asked to return to the same themes and cues for writing – autobiographical writing, reflections on conflict, research into particular topics – again and again through their education, and yet the nationally formulated model assumed a step-by-step progression, as many teachers promote in the teaching of Mathematics or modern foreign languages.

Arnold (1991) bases her recursive model of writing development on a four-year teacher-researcher study with 11- to 14-year-olds in Sydney. Her 'psychodynamic theory of writing development' assumes a spiral rather than a linear curriculum and 'an interest in the mind of the writer at work, not just an interest in the texts they produce' (p. 5). This interest in the writer is associated with a wider interest in what writing can do for a young person – 'the powerful psychological benefits which accrue from feeling centred in one's own exploratory writing and focusing on one's expressive needs' (ibid.). The focus on process rather than on product is indicative of a shift from the text to the writer that took place in the 1970s, 1980s and early 1990s, and marks what seems to be a generational pendulum swing between process and product.

One of the many valuable insights by Arnold is that there is more to writing than making marks on a page. All teachers have noted that sometimes writing assignments encourage a flow of writing and at other times the students can hardly scrape together a few words. Writing is a complex activity that draws on the imagination, feelings, state of mind, mood, cognitive state, capability with the medium, context and other factors. Her spiral model starts at a point which is the 'core self' and then moves up and away from that point, with the expressive self always at the centre of the spiral. The outer edges of the spiral touch different kinds of writing – the transactional, the poetic and other kinds (categories derived from the work of Britton in the 1970s) – as the writer increasingly widens the range of types of writing while at the same time holding on to the centrality of the self and the energy focused therein. Experience, contact with a range of audiences and self-reflection are as important as the kinds of writing they engender.

Critics of this approach would argue that the model is predicated on a single sense of self, and that young children have multiple selves that are expressible in a number of different ways; they would see models of writing development such as those by Britton and Arnold to be manifestations of a late Romantic approach to writing development, with the individual (supposedly integrated) self at the heart of the act of writing. Many others would see the approach as fundamental to the development of writers because it keys into their sense of purpose in the act of writing. Arnold's key point, I think, is that the integration of self that is possible through imaginative and well-thought-out writing activities justifies the act of writing; it 'expands writers' awareness of their expressive potential, centring them in a much larger universe of discourse' (1991: 32). Crucially,

> Self-reflection and reflexiveness are fundamental to self-development and the personalization of knowledge. Writing can play a part in the development of creative, integrated human beings who can afford to respect the uniqueness of themselves and of others because they have experienced their own capacity to make a mark in the world. (Ibid.)

'Making a mark' is a key phrase here, as writing is put alongside other graphic forms of expression (painting, multimedia creation) as extensions of human expressiveness.

Not all research is of this people-centred approach, however. Research into writing (rather than the writers and their motivation) has tended to focus on types of writing.

Narrative, argument and other modes of writing

One of the problems of discussing the research into writing 'above the level of the sentence' is definitional. Although terms like 'text' and 'context' are broad enough to denote a whole work and the location and function of that work in society and textual history, they themselves are subject to debate as to their boundaries. 'Text', for example, has been variously used to denote continuous passages of print, whole works, canonical works (as in 'set texts') and works in media other than print on a page: films, videos and other such 'media texts'. One of the advantages of using such a term is that the work in question can be analysed according to the principles of linguistic and semiotic study; another is that a commonality of approach can be used to bring together, often for comparison, works as diverse as newspaper journalism, poetry and documentary film. 'Context' can vary from the immediate and local to the distant and global; from the personal to the political; from ahistorical to historical; and from literary to linguistic.

One level below that of 'text' is the definition of kinds of text. There was much debate in the second half of the 1980s and first half of the 1990s about the nature of 'genre' in writing, particularly as it impinged upon the writing development of students in schools. Thinking in Australia was prompted by the Sydney School of linguists who tended to see genre as 'text type'; in Canada and the USA, the notion developed of 'genre as social action', that is of textual practice – for example, in the sociolegal development of a patent, as described by Bazerman (1988). In Britain, either there was little thinking along these lines or a resistance to classification, with teachers and researchers operating within the framework defined by Britton *et al.* (1975) of 'expressive', 'poetic' and 'transactional' writing.

Much research has taken place since the early 1980s on what might be termed the 'meta-genres' or modes of writing such as narrative, argument and (to a lesser extent in this unpoetic period) the lyric mode. In the late 1970s and 1980s, in the wake of studies in narrative form by linguists, anthropologists and literary and cultural critics, narrative established itself as the orthodoxy at the foundation of English work in schools. Storytelling (see Andrews, 1981), story-writing, the framing of talks, projects and other school genres in narrative form became widespread, particularly with the advent of 100 per cent coursework or portfolio assessment at 16 from the mid-1980s onwards. Narrative gained prominence not only as the basic mode of discourse from which all others might be generated, but also as the basic 'human paradigm' (Fisher, 1987). Claims were made by Rosen (1985) and others about the ubiquity of narrative and about its liberating presence in the curriculum; and in the USA, the telling of 'our stories' almost became a crusade in the 1990s, with minority ethnic groups embracing the genre as a means towards increased self-esteem, the reinforcement and discovery of identity and recognition from hegemonic powers in society. Narrative is unarguable; that is part of its power.

Research into story-grammars in the 1970s; (e.g. Rumelhart, 1975; Mandler and Johnson, 1977), however, has not translated easily into pedagogic practice in the classroom. Either the discourse grammars were too classificatory, or they were couched in arcane diction, or their function was to describe – and, indeed, their practical use seemed to turn out to be more in the field of Artificial Intelligence programming (i.e. logical or quasi-logical sequencing) rather than in the human domain.

In another study, Andrews (1992a) worked with a sample of 12/13-year-olds across a town in north-east England, experimenting with the use of sequences of photographs to generate written stories by students. This study hypothesized that students' difficulties in writing argument could be eased by basing their arguments on narrative structures with which they were more familiar. Although the study failed to prove such a connection, it did offer insights into the composing processes of writing narrative. These included the additive nature of composition in narrative in which the writer often did not know the outcome or shape of the narrative until he/she saw it emerge from the pen or wordprocessor; the reluctance to change the arrangement of the narrative once a first draft was committed to paper or screen; a facility to generate narrative from the sequencing of unconnected photographs, even by the academically weakest students; and a vast range of sequences demonstrated in a sample of over a hundred students, to the extent that no one narrative was similar in structure to any other. It is interesting to weigh these findings against those of Snyder (1991, 1993), who concluded from her research into writing approaches with computer and pen that students preferred the pen for narrative and the computer for argument. One of the reasons might be that the additive nature of composition in narrative is complemented by the more flowing, organic nature of writing with a pen; whereas the computer allows rearrangement of the macro-structure of the argument more readily.

For a full examination of the interface between narrative and argument, see Andrews, 1989.

Argument studies in education grew from work by Dixon and Stratta for the then Southern Examining Board in the early 1980s. Their line was basically that argument had been taught in schools in an academic way: the emphasis was on balance, the putting of points for and against followed by a dispassionate summing up of the case at the end. Such conventions led to formulaic approaches to argument in the essay – the 'default genre' in education according to Womack (1993) – like stating what you are going to do, doing it and then telling the reader what you have done. To break the conventions, Dixon and Stratta encouraged writers in school to advocate arguments rather than rehearse others' arguments. Topics were suggested that had more relevance to young people, like whether to allow longer recesses and break-times in the summer terms or semesters; whether or not to site a road-safety crossing outside school; whether uniforms should be compulsory and whether boys and girls should be treated differently in this respect. The drive was to recognize the political life of young people and to make the genres in which they were asked to write more responsive to their voices and their needs.

The shift away from academic adversarial argument towards advocative argument heralded another shift: towards an understanding that argument could be consensual as well as adversarial (see Costello and

Mitchell, 1995). Some critics argued that such a move might be seen as part of a larger feminist movement away from male-dominated discourse; Berrill, for example, offered metaphors of dance to describe the operation of argument in order to counter the prevailing metaphors of war and battle, journey and construction. It seems to me, however, that different models of argument cannot be successfully characterized in polarized gender terms, as suggested in the work of Tannen (1998) and others. Rather, a more sensitive analysis would depict the different kinds of argument as existing on a spectrum of possibility, from the fiercely adversarial on the one hand (as evidenced in some parliaments, in media debates (see Litosseliti, 1999)), to consensual development on the other (e.g. discourse in counselling, the elicitation of argumentative positions through inductive storytelling).

One of the studies which focused on argument in the classroom was by Andrews *et al.* (1993), a report on a two-year action research project with teachers in ten primary and ten secondary schools in eastern England. The work is summarized in Andrews (1995). What the research revealed was that young children – for example, those aged five to seven – are capable of extended and fairly sophisticated argumentation in speech. There are examples of group discussion and role-play in which children take an idea and provide both evidence and counter-evidence for it; in which they challenge propositions; in which they generate new propositions and claims from existing ones; in which they move both toward consensus and away from it. Role-play, in particular, was a device which liberated children to explore the development of argument, aided by structural cues such as 'Can I just ask you something about that . . .?', 'Are you saying that . . .?', 'What if . . .?' and 'I don't agree with you about that point'. The 'what if?' question is interesting: it suggests that argument is as much driven by scenario-building and hypothesizing – and thus by the imagination – as narrative and creative work.

Grammar

Perhaps the first point to make in this section is that made by Perera:

> Since the beginning of the century, a body of research has accumulated that indicates that grammatical instruction, unrelated to pupils' other language work, does not lead to an improvement in the quality of their own writing or in the level of their

comprehension. Furthermore, the majority of children under about fourteen seem to become confused by grammatical labels and descriptions. It is obviously harmful for children to be made to feel that they 'can't do English' because they cannot label, say, an auxiliary verb, when they are perfectly capable of using a wide range of auxiliary verbs accurately and appropriately. (1984: 12)

She cites Wilkinson (1971) for a brief summary of research into this topic.

Two books by Perera (1984, 1987) provide a foundation for studies in grammar and language awareness in education. The second of these, *Understanding Language*, is a useful starting point, as it discusses knowledge about language which in turn is divided into three different kinds of knowledge: first, 'the implicit knowledge that all native speakers have' (p. 2); second, the explicit knowledge about the nature and functions of the language, including how it is acquired, how and why it varies and changes; third, 'there is explicit knowledge of the structure of language – knowledge which includes the technical terminology necessary to describe the production and organization of speech sounds, the relationships of meaning between different words, and the grammatical structures of the language' (ibid.). Perera's 1987 paper touches on the issue that is at the heart of much of the controversy about teaching grammar and/or language awareness. She makes a distinction between what teachers need to know and what they need to teach. *Academic* study of the language for its own sake is something she sees, rightly, as a fascinating topic, but as an optional area of study at the later stages of schooling – for example, in advanced level English study, which is possible in the UK.

One aspect of language awareness teachers need to have is how much language children bring to school at the age of five or six. Early language acquisition is a field in itself (see, for example, Ervin-Tripp and Mitchell-Kernan, 1977), and children's capability is often underestimated at the start of formal schooling because the situation they find themselves in is different from those they are used to; their language may sometimes seem impoverished because they cannot speak with the same fluency that they enjoy in other contexts. Perera (1987) draws the important distinction between accent, dialect and spoken standard English, making the point that there are a number of standard Englishes around the world and that spoken standard English in England and Wales, say, refers only to grammar and vocabulary, not to pronunciation. This last point is reinforced in her statement that 'a regional dialect will always be spoken in a regional accent; but [spoken] standard English can be spoken in Received Pronunciation or in a regional accent' (p. 9). It is likely that the term 'received pronunciation' with its association with 'BBC English' or 'a proper accent' will fade in use, assuming as it does a 'correct' way of speaking. Although there may well continue to be a socially agreed 'norm' or approved accent, the notion of 'received pronunciation' as standard is under attack, and has been for many years. The term 'spoken standard English' seems to have gained ascendancy, with the clear indication that it is not a spoken version of written standard English, but a dialect and accent in its own right. The orthodox position on language use at present, at least in English curricula in England, is that expressed by Perera (1987) thus: whereas students will use English with an accent of some kind, there is no reason for schools to attempt to alter that accent as long as the speech is comprehensible; but 'what does matter . . . is grammar: what is at issue is whether children who habitually speak one of the regional varieties of English can also use the grammar of standard English when it is appropriate' (p. 10).

Before I go on to discuss the place of grammar and language awareness in English teaching, it has to be said that in a pluralist and diverse society, there can be disagreements even with Perera's balanced conclusion that all children should be able to 'use the grammar of standard English when it is appropriate'. The two main objections are that the grammar of spoken English needs to be distinguished from the grammar of written English (as Perera does); and that 'appropriateness' is a matter for social groups to decide for themselves, not for a hegemony to decide.

Leaving that debate for other occasions, it is worth recording Perera's view that explicit teaching about the language is best delayed until the third or fourth year of junior school (i.e. ages 9–11) and that the encouragement to use spoken standard English in some situations is best left to ages 13–15, when social demands and an understanding of the different nature of social situations become clearer and more critical to young people. In another section of the paper, Perera (1987) suggests that although children bring a great deal of language awareness and competence to school when they first arrive, they continue to develop these through the primary and secondary years.

One of the conclusions to draw from Perera's research is similar to that drawn with regard to the teaching of spelling: that equipping students with the tools to investigate language is as important as teaching them the rules and systems that underpin it. A classroom that encourages discussion and debate about language will engender the kind of interest that makes a student wish to find out more and to make the distinctions that are important to a sophisticated use of the language. Another conclusion is that 'it is essential to recognize that language is too complex to be handled by a series of prescriptions or, more often, proscriptions. A more valid alternative is to provide guidelines rather than rules; saying, for example, "Think carefully about . . ." rather than "Never . . .".' And in terms of the terminology required to understand language and to contribute to the better use of it, both in speech and in writing, Perera suggests that it is helpful if primary and secondary teachers have sufficient command 'to be able to read books written for teachers about children's language' (p. 37) and that knowledge of technical terms can help in the identification of students' strengths and weaknesses – beyond a basic vocabulary of key terms, other terms are not necessary unless they illuminate aspects of the process of writing or are used diagnostically to help students understand how to improve.

Sentence structure, which is what grammars attempt to describe, can be taught simply and with a lighter touch than is implied by the 'naming of parts'. In order to distinguish between and be able to use simple, compound and complex sentences, the following activity has been proved to be effective at many levels in education. First, a simple sentence is presented, like 'The cow jumped over the moon.' It is *simple* because of the subject–verb–object construction. The sentence can be made into a compound one by using a conjunction: 'The cow jumped over the moon *and* fell on the other side.' From a compound structure like this one – or indeed from a simple structure, a complex sentence can be constructed: '*While I was watching the cormorants skim across the surface of the sea*, the cow jumped over the moon and fell on the other side.' The fact that the newly added words constitute a relative clause need or need not be the subject of discussion in the class: such a decision depends on the level of the class and the level of interest in language. My point is that the term *clause* is not necessary for the creation of the sentence, or for its further development, as in '*On Sunday*, while I was watching the cormorants skim *like flat, black stones* across the surface of the *implacable* sea, the *brown* cow jumped over the moon and fell on the other side, *into darkness.*' And so on.

The question does arise in activities like this as to whether one needs to know the basic guidelines for the construction of a sentence in order to judge how best to build upon what is there in simple form. Put another way, Her Majesty's Inspectorate for schools noted in the early 1980s a problem with sentence structure in the writing of large cohorts of students at sixteen and younger in England and Wales. It identified the 'run-on sentence' or 'comma splice' as the heart of the problem. Such 'sentences' as 'I walked home early yesterday, the door was locked when I got there' can be simply solved by starting a new sentence: 'I walked home early yesterday. The door was locked when I got there'; or by using a semi-colon: 'I walked home early yesterday; the door was locked when I got there'; or by using a conjunction: 'I walked home early yesterday but the door was locked when I got there.' My conclusion, like Perera's, is that developing an ear and an eye for grammatical propriety and variation is a better guide to the writing of English than an over-reliance on rules – most of which are either too difficult to formulate and remember or are invalidated by too many exceptions.

A much fuller account of grammatical analysis, the acquisition of grammar, differences between speech and writing and the development of children's writing at a number of levels is to be found in Perera's book *Children's Writing and Reading* (1984). Hudson's *Teaching Grammar* (1992) takes a more pragmatic line, covering standard English and the politics of grammar teaching in England and providing both an 'encyclopedia' of grammar (an extensive and full glossary) and 'some grammar lessons'.

Perera (1984) notes how important it is to have some knowledge of grammatical construction in English in order to be able to make efficient use of the marking of and responding to students' written work that takes up much of English teachers' time. Vague responses by teachers who do not get at the heart of grammatical problems in students' work are of little help, as they do not address the problems and simply leave the door open for more errors of the same kind to recur. Teachers 'should have the ability to [undertake grammatical analysis] when the need arises' (p. 10). She notes the difference, however, between descriptive grammars of the language, like Quirk *et al.* (1972), and generative grammars arising from the seminal work of Chomsky (1964, 1965) and others. Her approach is based on the former, because generative grammars do not, on the whole, provide the basis for developmental studies so important to education – particularly in that their account of complexity (the generation of complexity in sentence structure from simple core utterances) does not match either the production or development of grammatical complexity in children and young people.

Hudson (1992) characterizes the problem of teaching and learning grammar and language awareness as approaching the problem from two different directions. Traditionally, descriptive grammar was taught, from a top-down or deductive perspective. That is to say, first the grammar was defined by linguists in all its terminological and classificatory diversity, with local rules, exceptions and the like. Then it was 'taught' to classes of children who had to 'parse' sentences and deal with dislocated and fragmented chunks of (largely, written) language. The other direction, reflecting education principles and values of a different kind, could be said to be 'bottom-up' or inductive: from this perspective, children explored examples of real language in order to generate rules and patterns which they might apply, by analogy, to other examples of language. The inductive approach is more attuned to learning needs; the deductive to teaching programmes. The best balance is somewhere in between these two poles, with informed teachers using pedagogically sensitive techniques to elicit learning on the part of their students. As Hudson puts it, the new approach

> is based on discovery-learning of grammar in which the child's own non-standard spoken language is just as relevant as written Standard English, and the aim is just as much to deepen the child's awareness of what it already knows and does as to help the child to learn Standard English. It combines a liberal respect for the child's values with the hard-nosed aim of raising standards, in the belief that the former will in fact support the latter. (1992: 14)

It is impossible to summarize the range and complexity of the discussions of the role of grammar and language awareness in writing (and reading) development in children and young people. Those interested in answers to particular grammatical problems or more generally in children's development in writing are referred to Perera (1984), Kress's *Learning to Write* (1994) and Wilkinson *et al.*'s *Assessing Language Development* (1980), the last of which is discussed in more detail later in this chapter.

Punctuation

Punctuation is a surface feature or skill determined by the ability to think in and structure sentences. In other words, it is hard to know how to punctuate unless you know what you want to say and how you want to say it. At the same time, those who are weak at punctuation and struggle with full stops, commas and capital letters are not only finding it difficult to put meaning on paper; they are also using these basic marks to fulfil the functions of other, less used marks – the semi-colon, the colon, hyphens, dashes, parentheses – and so compounding the problems for themselves as writers. As Shaughnessy puts it:

> Limited mainly to commas and periods [full stops], the inexperienced writer is further restricted by his uncertain use of these marks: commas appear at odd junctures within sentences, and both commas and periods mark off sentence terminations, or what appear to be terminations, for the writer frequently mistakes a fragment for a whole sentence or joins two sentences with a comma (comma splice) or with no punctuation at all (run-on). (1977: 17)

Shaughnessy's views concur with the general line in this book, namely that it is difficult to teach such skills in isolation. Rather, 'the study of punctuation ought not to begin with the marks themselves but with the structures that elicit these marks; first, with the recognition and creation of simple subject and predicate phrases; second, with the embedding of sentences within sentences . . .; third, with the embedding of appositional forms; and fourth, with the embedding of *–ing* phrases' (1977: 29). Essentially, then, Shaughnessy reminds us that

> punctuation is a response to sentence structure. It does not initiate forms so much as supply them in the wake of larger choices that affect the way a sentence is shaped. And if this is so, then the study of punctuation ought to be a study of sentence structure, not merely a definition of the marks themselves. To remind a student repeatedly that a period is used at the end of a sentence and then to illustrate this with a few isolated sentences is valueless if he is confused about sentence boundaries. What he needs is a sequence of lessons with accompanying exercises that clarify what is going on in sentences so that the rules of punctuation can be consistently applied. (1977: 40–1)

Spelling

There are two main problems in learning to spell: one is the complexity of the English spelling system, and the other is the range of techniques required in order to gain command of this system. Torbe (1977) set out a balanced approach which drew on a wide number of strategies, ranging from grapho-phonemic equivalence ('sounding out the word') to morphological approaches (parts of words) and from visual memory to the various rules (none of them absolute) that underpin the spelling system in English. His book is still a useful basis from which to devise a strategy for teaching and learning spelling. Published in the same year was Shaughnessy's landmark study of the errors made by college writing students in New York, *Errors and Expectations* (1977), mentioned above with regard to punctuation, which, through an analysis of students' writing, strove to reconceive 'errors' as attempts to re-create meaning on the page against (in many cases) huge odds. She reminds us that 'in teaching inexperienced writers to write we are usually contending not with a number of discrete difficulties . . . but with a central condition of ill-preparedness with formal written language' (p. 161):

> This condition pervades all the sub-systems of that skill, producing errors that may be classified under different headings in a composition handbook but that nonetheless rise from a common ground: from the student's rootedness in spoken rather than written language and his habitual preference for forms of English that diverge in a variety of ways from formal English; from a general lack of visual acuity and memory in relation to the written letter and word patterns; from the student's efforts to simulate a register or code he is not sure of; and finally from an urge to move into deep grammatical and lexical waters in the effort to communicate complex thoughts. (p. 161)

Shaughnessy identifies misspellings caused by unpredictabilities within the English spelling system, those caused by pronunciation or homophonic equivalence, misspellings caused by unfamiliarity with the structure of words and those caused by failure to see or remember words. Her suggestions for improving spelling can be set out as follows. (Readers who wish for a more detailed account are advised to consult *Errors and Expectations* itself.)

1. Assume at the outset that the misspellings of young adults can be brought under control;
2. begin by teaching the student to observe himself as a speller;
3. before attempting to work on individual errors, make certain that the student understands certain terms and operations;
4. if possible start to work on misspellings that can be controlled by the application of rules;
5. develop an awareness of the main discrepancies between the student's pronunciation of words and the models of pronunciation upon which the spelling system is based;
6. develop an awareness of the ways in which pronunciation helps the speller;
7. develop the student's ability to discriminate among graphemic options;
8. develop precision in viewing written words;
9. teach the use of the dictionary.

In a report for the TTA as part of its scheme to promote teacher research, Sowerby (1999) investigated the medium-term effectiveness of raising spelling achievement through a cued spelling approach with a class of 10–11-year-old children. Cued spelling 'is a multi-sensory approach' in which children are trained by the teacher to work in pairs: one as the *helper* and one as the *speller*. The helper 'assists the speller in learning how to spell words, following a ten-step procedure. At the end of each session, the helper gives the speller a test to assess the short term recall of the day's spellings' (p. 2). The ten steps, as described by Sowerby, are:

1. pupils select a word to learn/are given target words;
2. pairs check correct spelling using a dictionary, and enter the word in their spelling diaries;
3. pairs read the word together; the speller reads the word alone;
4. speller and helper choose cue together;
5. pairs repeat cue aloud;
6. speller says cue while helper writes word;
7. helper says cue while speller writes word;
8. speller writes word quickly and says cue aloud;
9. speller writes word quickly;
10. speller reads word aloud.

Initial studies of the cued spelling approach showed mean gains of 0.69 a year in terms of spelling age per child (Marlin, 1997). Sowerby's study found that children in both the project group and the control group improved their spelling scores during the period of the research, and that there was no significant difference between the two groups – neither in spelling scores nor after the analysis of creative writing by both groups. However, within the project group 'the *helpers'* spelling attainment continued to improve during the six months after the intervention, whereas the *spellers'* test scores remained the same as they had done at the end of the intervention period' (Sowerby, 1999: 3). The general implication from both studies is that self-esteem and confidence in an area of knowledge is a crucial factor in making advances in that area. It is also a worrying research implication, in that it does not answer how best to help those children who have difficulties in learning.

One of the spin-offs from Sowerby's research gives a clue as to what strategies might be useful to help weaker spellers. Students who participated in the experimental group in her research were more confident about the spellings they knew and also 'about ways of finding out and learning new spellings' (Sowerby, 1999: 3). In other words, they had developed strategies for problem-solving to aid their learning of spelling, and had moved beyond the sounding out of words as their only strategy. The new ways of finding out included increased independent use of dictionaries; circling difficult parts of words; analogy with other similar words; and visual memory of whole words.

In another relatively small-scale study, Daw *et al.* (1997) surveyed nine primary schools in Suffolk, England, where results for spelling in national tests in 1994 and 1995 were particularly high. Possible factors underlying good spelling performance were identified and these ran to an extensive list, including general linguistic experience, the structure of the teaching programme, quality of teaching, resources, the way individual children learned spellings, marking and assessment practices, home–school links and special educational needs practice. In the course of the research itself, it emerged that there were dominant factors across the sample. These were:

- general linguistic experience: displays of spelling, alphabet, key words, topic words and letter strings; an interest in language which manifests itself in discussion about words in the context of reading and writing;

- structure of the teaching programme: understanding and consistent use of a few key strategies, approaches or schemes; the early and systematic teaching of phonics; the extensive use of rhymes in the early years; effective early reading;
- early but systematic moves through the first stages of writing, with a balance between goal and structure;
- a systematic approach to covering major spelling regularities 'which includes teaching and discussion, learning words and assessing progress through regular testing'. (Daw *et al.*, 1997: 42)

One important finding was that although the use of a weekly list was common to many schools, the addition of words to the list by students helped spark an interest in words and develop some of the analogical strategies that are so helpful in spelling. For example, a word list that included *actual, eventual* and *effectual* might invite students to provide words such as *visual, virtual* and *punctual* – and if students offered words that did not fit this pattern, useful discussion could be had as to how the differences were manifested and how to remember them.

Other factors were:

- the quality of teaching and use of resources: regular brief instruction sessions to whole classes, with appropriate differentiation within a context of high expectation for all pupils;
- the way individual students learn and record spellings: encouraging experimentation and independence from an early age;
- regular marking of students' work, with the indication of some spelling errors as one part of the feedback provided to students to help them improve.

It is clear that it is dispiriting to receive written work back from a teacher with no attention to content or structure or style, but merely the marking of spelling and punctuation errors in red pen. Such marking needs to include constructive approaches to improving spelling, like the identification of patterns and a systematic and *manageable* number of spellings to work on.

The final factor mentioned in the Daw *et al.* (1997) study is the importance of home–school links, with a clear explanation by the school of the ways in which parents or guardians can help their children to improve.

Snowling *et al.*'s (1996) research will be discussed in Chapter 4 in relation to dyslexia in reading. As far as the spelling of children with dyslexic reading difficulties goes, in the first two years of the study,

> [t]he dyslexic children . . . made less progress in spelling words of one to four syllables than did the normal readers over the 2 years they were studied. By [the end of the two years] the younger normal readers had gone further in mastering alphabetic spelling strategies, whereas the dyslexic children continued to make a high proportion of phonetically inaccurate spelling errors. These results suggest that one of the reasons that the dyslexic children were improving less well than the normal readers was their difficulties with the use of phonological spelling strategies. (p. 666)

The assessment of writing

Drawing on models of English such as that presented in Moffett (1968) and Britton *et al.* (1975), Wilkinson *et al.* (1980) studied the development of written language in 7- to 14-year-olds, suggesting that the usual criteria for judging writing were too narrow, and that teachers needed to take into account such factors as the emotional, moral and cognitive development of the children behind the texts, as it were. As the authors describe the experiment ('The Crediton Project'), 'four different kinds of composition – narrative, autobiographical, explanatory and argumentative – were requested from groups of children at seven, ten and thirteen respectively, in the context of their normal lessons. The same four subjects were given to each group so that the compositions could be more easily compared' (p. 2). The authors set out the four models used to serve as systems of analysis – in the fields of cognition, affect, morals and style:

> *Cognitive* The basis of this model is a movement from an undifferentiated world to a world organized by mind, from a world of instances to a world related by generalities and abstractions.
>
> *Affective* Development is seen as being in three movements – one towards a greater awareness of self, a second towards a greater awareness of neighbour as self, a third towards an inter-engagement of reality and imagination.

Moral 'Anomy' or lawlessness gives way to 'heteronomy' or rule by fear of punishment, which in turn gives way to 'socionomy' or rule by a sense of reciprocity with others which finally leads to the emergence of 'autonomy' or self-rule.

Stylistic Development is seen as choices in relation to a norm of the simple, literal, affirmative sentence which characterizes children's early writing. Features such as structure, cohesion, verbal competence, syntax, reader awareness, sense of appropriateness, undergo modification. (pp. 2–3)

From an early twenty-first century perspective, these models appear informed by Piagetian theories of development; nevertheless, as Wilkinson *et al.* (1980) point out, 'there was scarcely any previous work to go on' as far as the second and fourth categories were concerned. The main point – and one which continues to endure – is of a holistic and carefully calibrated model for gauging development in writing.

Implications for practice

As with learning to read, the range of research on writing is extensive and the implications arising from the research are manifold. Writing research has moved in the last thirty years or so from an interest in the products of writing (and resultant categorization of different types of writing) through an interest in the processes of writing (resulting in planning and drafting) to two current preoccupations: the nature of writing on-screen, and the locations and acts of writing in schools and wider communities.

The implications for practice in the teaching of writing, arising from a critical review of research in the field, are:

- young people need opportunities for extended writing in a number of different genres and text-types;
- they should write on-screen, on paper and with a variety of tools for writing; and reflect upon the different nature of each of these approaches to writing;
- the distinction between composition and the 'secretarial skills' needs to be made clear, so that young people are not inhibited by surface constraints when they are composing (particularly in the early years); on the other hand, editing skills need to be taught so that the 'secretarial' capabilities are developed;

- school writing needs to find an increasing range of real audiences;
- the closer writing in school approximates a dialogue – whether with the teacher, others in the school or those outside school – the more engaging it will be to reluctant writers;
- writing, and the history of writing, needs to be celebrated in school so that it is appreciated as a major strand of civilization;
- there needs to be a wide range of approaches to the teaching of spelling;
- teaching grammar is often counterproductive; but teaching language awareness and sentence structure via the embedding method are productive.

Chapter 4

Reading

Of the research resources underpinning all the chapters in this book, the research literature on reading is probably the most extensive. Not only researchers into the education process, but those with an interest in psychology, cognitive development, semiotics and linguistics have all found the business of learning to read to be central to some of their investigations. In addition, reading is seen to be the foundational capability in the acquisition of literacy. Although its reciprocity with learning to write is rarely acknowledged fully, it is generally assumed (often falsely) that reading precedes writing capability. The 'literacy hour' which was introduced to English and Welsh primary schools in 1998, although ostensibly about learning to read and write, privileges reading over writing. A third factor contributing to the importance of reading are the increased demands society places on young people to be able to read to survive. It is a truism to say that expectations of literacy increased during the twentieth century for the mass of populations in countries around the world; but it is also true to say that the information and communication technology revolution has added to such expectations. Within the confines of the present book, what is offered here is a selection and distillation of the research into reading.

Before exploring some of the research into reading, it is necessary to set out a map of what is involved in learning to read, so that particular examples of research can be placed relative to others. Becoming a competent reader involves gaining command of each of the levels at which the written code operates. From the smallest to the largest unit, these are: the grapho-phonemic level (the relationship between letters and sounds in the English language), the morphological level (morphemes are parts of words), the lexical level (words themselves), the syntactic level (how words are combined to make phrases, clauses and sentences – also called the 'grammatical' level), the sub-textual level (paragraphs, stanzas – building blocks in the creation and analysis of whole texts), the textual level (whole works, ranging from poems to essays to reports to stories and so on) and the contextual level (including historical, generic and linguistic as well as socio-political contexts).

The Bullock Report: standards of reading attainment

Much of the Bullock Report[1] (1975) is devoted to reading. Indeed, understanding the nature of and problems associated with reading might be said to be the bedrock of the extensive and influential report. The Committee of Inquiry which was set up under Sir Alan Bullock's chairmanship was announced after the publication of the National Foundation for Educational Research's report *The Trend of Reading Standards*, but as the introduction to the DES report notes, 'reading was not singled out for special attention but was placed in close association with other language skills within the context of teaching the use of English' (p. xxxi). Another central principle, stated early in the report, is that 'there is no one method, medium, approach, device or philosophy that holds the key to the process of learning to read' (p. xxxii). The general approach, therefore, is one that in the USA has come to be known as 'whole language'; that is to say, it conceives of language development as being an organic whole, rooted in the contexts in which young people find themselves and with speaking, listening, reading and writing (we might add from the current perspective the act of 'viewing') informing each other. Another aspect of whole language approaches is that they do not compartmentalize the act of learning into 'key stages' or phases, preferring to see development as seamless and not necessarily steady or regulated.

A point made early in the report is that it is impossible to determine whether reading standards rose or fell in the post-war generation. Pre-war tests were not standardized. A report, *Progress in Reading 1948–1964*, (Department of Education and Science, 1966) suggested that there had been an advance of seventeen months of reading age for 11-year-olds and twenty to thirty months for 15-year-olds; but as the Bullock Report comments:

Not all reviewers have agreed that this represents what the [HMI] report described as a 'remarkable improvement'. Several pointed out that the 1948 test scores were naturally depressed as a result of the war and that they therefore presented a low base-line which would flatter subsequent results. (p. 15)

The factors affecting the interpretation of reading test results are many and varied, their interrelationship complex, and pages 16–19 of the Bullock Report give a clear account of why we should treat all such results with a great deal of caution. While tests can be devised that are highly *reliable* in that they measure consistently, it is very difficult to devise a test which is *valid* in that it gives a full account of the complexity of reading achievement. Some of the factors or variables which change over time, for instance, include the language itself and the access of young people to particular aspects of the language; the range of ability of young people taking the tests; sociological determinants; and the understanding of how the different levels of language interrelate in the process and achievement of reading. Despite all these caveats, however, Bullock was able to summarize that, in the light of surveys in the late 1960s and early 1970s, there was no significant change in the overall reading standards of 11-year-olds over the decade 1960–1970, but that the proportion of poor readers in the unskilled and semi-skilled social groups was growing. At 15 years of age reading standards remained 'approximately the same' during the period after a post-war period of steady increase, though Bullock warned that taking the 1948 records as a baseline was unsatisfactory, for reasons mentioned earlier. The Report's recommendations that 'a new system of monitoring should be introduced' (p. 26) was realized in the establishment of the Assessment of Performance Unit, the terms of reference for which were set out in 1974. The aim of the APU was to provide solid evidence of standards and to depend less on anecdotal evidence to inform policy and practice. The next national survey of reading capability was undertaken by APU between 1979 and 1983 (see Thornton, 1987). Between these dates, ten surveys were carried out, five with primary pupils aged 11 and five with secondary pupils aged 15: a total of 47,000 primary and 45,000 secondary pupils in all.

One of the key findings of the 1982 Primary Survey (APU, 1982) was that reading 'necessarily involves a process of formulating hypotheses' (Thornton, 1987: 16):

It is characteristic of the poor readers that while they quite certainly form hypotheses, are active readers, and make some sort of sense in relation to what they read, they do not appear to be consistently alert to the need to revise their 'readings' and to monitor their own interpretation against the text. (APU, 1982: 147)

Such surveys led on, in due course and indirectly, to the National Curriculum test scores at 7, 11 and 14. These have run from the early 1990s to the present in England and Wales, but not without controversy and changing goalposts.

In a relatively recent article, Hunter-Grundin (1997) notes no drop in reading standards for 7- to 12-year-olds between 1979 and 1996, but a widening performance gap between middle-class and 'low income' schools, thus confirming the suspicions of the Bullock Committee in the mid-1970s. Hunter-Grundin's research is based on application of the Hunter/Grundin Reading-for-Meaning Scales, first standardized in 1979 with a large (2,500+) sample for each of five tests, and providing a clear benchmark for national 'reading standards' at the time. The procedure largely consists of modified cloze tests. Restandardization took place in 1996 after a survey of 5,138 pupils in 44 different schools in the UK. Hunter-Grundin's results confirm those of other national surveys, namely that there has been no significant rise or fall in the standards of reading in the 7–12 age group in England (and the rest of the UK) in the last twenty to twenty-five years, and that concerns about reading standards are more likely to be due to increased expectations of reading ability. As she points out, 'the most striking finding is that the gap between middle-class and "low-income" schools in 1996 is much wider than it was in 1979. Expressed in Reading Age terms, the difference between these two groups amounts to one year and three months at [age 7+] and to a full two years at [age 11+]. In other words, the gap . . . has more than doubled' during the period.

If reading failure is to be addressed at all, it seems then that societal differentiation will be *the* major factor. The elimination of exclusion from the fabric of society will be a prerequisite for improvement in the overall standard of reading. The Labour government elected in 1997 put social inclusion high on its agenda, but at the same time proceeded with an educational policy – 'raising standards' – that, fuelled by the Office for Standards in Education (Ofsted), targeted teachers with the task of implementing government policy in education, the flagship of which, at primary level at least, was the 'literacy hour'. Hilton (1998) attacks the appropriation of teacher creativity and independence in the imposition of this 'hour', which consisted of 40 minutes of teacher talk (instruction, questioning, cajoling, etc.) and 20 minutes of directed small group work, leaving little space in the curriculum for extended reading or writing. She reveals that the research base for this policy implementation was itself insubstantial, depending heavily on Ofsted reports and 1995 and 1996 end-of-key-stage results for 7-year-olds; and also on an Ofsted report, *The Teaching of Reading in 45 Inner London Primary Schools*, the methodology of which was critiqued by Mortimore and Goldstein (1996) – both of which are discussed in more detail in the next section.

Rather than formulaic solutions like the literacy hour, the underlying social factors behind the long tail of pupils who achieved scores well below the average – a phenomenon that we have seen replicated in studies from the 1970s onwards – need to be addressed. Hilton cites Robinson (1997) who concludes, after a survey of key longitudinal reports, that social disadvantage is the key factor in impeding key skills development, and that 'there is no evidence from these longitudinal studies that such factors as primary school class size, teaching methods, homework policy or the use of streaming or setting has any impact on the attainment of literacy or numeracy' (Hilton, 1998: 10). The two factors that do help attainment in literacy are, according to these authors, peer-group effect, where there is a mix of children from different class backgrounds within the same learning community; and the degree of parental interest and involvement in their child's education. Schools, however good they are, cannot eliminate the differential between socially advantaged and disadvantaged groups. What is needed, advocates Hilton, is a richer understanding of the relationship between literacy and culture, and the need for teachers to be ethnographers of their pupils' community literacy, rather than to impose a model which in turn has been imposed on them.

Barnes (1993), in her review of the development of national tests at 14 for students in England and Wales, gives an account of the difficulty of creating an assessment system to gauge reading and writing capability, particularly in a climate where end-of-year or end-of-stage tests were beginning to drive the curriculum. The problem with such tests, argues Barnes, is that the assessment of reading is through the tangibility of what the student writes or says; it is impossible to measure what is going on inside the student's head as he or she reads. Even then, she writes, 'our judgement is subjective, since it rests largely on whether the pupil's understanding accords with our own. In any case, the very idea of testing reading by short written tests runs counter to both common sense and to stress placed by the National Curriculum on range and variety [of reading matter]' (p. 7). Her story of the frequent changes and increasing narrowness and prescriptiveness of tests for reading proved to set a pattern for the 1990s that has carried over into the twenty-first century, with teacher assessment taking second place to 'end-of-key-stage tests' to measure literacy development in 7-, 11- and 14-year-olds in their passage towards the general public examinations at 16.

What can we say, in summary, about reading standards in young people in the half-century or so since reliable records were kept? First, that tests are changed every ten to fifteen years in the light of the changing contexts for reading. Second, that expectations of what it means to be literate are rising, year on year. Third, that girls have made better progress overall than boys during the period. Fourth, that the overall standard has probably improved, but not as fast as the expectations have soared. The gap between expectation and actuality has therefore widened.

The teaching of reading

In 1996, two reports were published on the state of reading in a number of primary schools in London: Ofsted's *The Teaching of Reading in 45 Inner London Primary Schools* (1996) and a critique of that report by Peter Mortimore and Harvey Goldstein, *The Teaching of Reading in 45 Inner London Primary Schools: A Critical Examination of Ofsted Research* (1996).

The Ofsted report was based on inspections in Year 2 (6/7-year-olds) and Year 6 (10/11-year-olds) in 15 schools in each of the London Boroughs of Islington, Tower Hamlets and Southwark – chosen because of their poor literacy results in National Curriculum test scores and in public examinations at school-leaving age (16). Two sources of evidence were gathered: one-day inspections of each of the schools by Ofsted inspectors and local teaching authority advisers; and a common test of reading administered by the National Foundation for Educational Research at Year 2 and at Year 6. Some of the main findings were that:

- weaknesses in teaching hampered pupils' progress and attainment in reading in one in three lessons in Year 2 and nearly half of the lessons in Year 6;
- the teaching of phonic knowledge and skills was often insufficient and of poor quality. Some aspects of phonic knowledge and skills were taught in Year 2, but teaching was usually limited to letter–sound correspondences. Direct, systematic teaching of phonic work was relatively rare, especially in Year 6 where many pupils continued to need such teaching;
- the teaching of higher order and information skills in Year 6 was, with few exceptions, weak;
- listening to individual pupils read was the principal strategy used by most teachers for teaching reading in Year 2. In many cases, however, this simply became an unproductive routine exercise of such short duration that very little actual teaching took place. The effective teaching of pupils in groups, and especially as a whole class, about specific aspects of reading was uncommon;
- black African pupils performed better than other ethnic groups at both Year 2 and Year 6. Bangladeshi pupils achieved low scores in Year 2 but performed better in Year 6. White pupils from economically disadvantaged backgrounds consistently performed least well and constituted the largest group of underachievers in Year 6;

Ofsted (1996) suggested that urgent action needed to be taken by the schools and education authorities to train teachers (both pre- and in-service) in the teaching of reading, 'with a clear emphasis on phonics' (p. 10); headteachers were to play a more prominent role in monitoring the progress in reading in their pupils and in undertaking the appraisal of newly qualified teachers in the teaching of reading; and suitable policies needed to be laid down, especially to link the teaching of reading to writing, speaking and listening.

Mortimore and Goldstein (1996) criticize the Ofsted report on a number of fronts. First, they suggest that the Neale Analysis of Reading Ability test (the test used by NFER on reading ability and reading comprehension) was last revised in the late 1980s 'so that its relevance to reading in the mid-1990s is debatable' (p. 3); that 'given that the sample was selected to represent children from highly disadvantaged backgrounds, it can be no surprise that reading levels in the sample are lower than the national average' (ibid.); and that 'serious doubts have been voiced about the validity of the standardization' (ibid.). Second, Mortimore and Goldstein point out that in comparing progress between Year 2 and Year 6,

> Investigators had to make an assumption that the intakes to the schools had not varied much over the last four years and that the two groups of pupils were likely to be fairly similar. This assumption, which buttresses the main conclusions of the Report, is, in fact, highly dubious . . . (p. 5)

Indeed, many of the interpretations by Ofsted of the data collected are questioned by Mortimore and Goldstein, including claims that the wide gulf in pupils' reading performances is serious and unacceptable; that individual reading tuition could be replaced by more effective group and whole class teaching; that phonics contributed to the accuracy and fluency of reading by children of all abilities; and that a limited number of schools emerged as more or less effective than others. Mortimore and Goldstein (p. 7) suggest that 'It is now well established that a necessary condition for passing any kind of judgement concerning the relative effectiveness of schools requires longitudinal follow-up information on the same group of pupils.' Furthermore, Ofsted's claims about effectiveness cannot be sustained because there is no intake data upon which to make a baseline judgement. Its claim that findings from the inner London study are generalizable are also criticized for being ill judged, and the clarity and transparency of the presentation of results is questioned. Along with other objections to the methodology and tone (its 'negative spin'), the critique concludes that the Ofsted report 'as an exercise . . . fell between inspection and research and carried out neither task satisfactorily' (p. 9).

The Bullock Report: the nature of reading

The Bullock Report was very anxious to point out the false conflict between those who see learning to read as a process of converting print into sounds ('decoding') and those who see such decoding as 'taking second place to securing and expanding the child's interest, keeping his curiosity alive, and giving reading a meaning' (p. 77), sometimes characterized as 'bringing meaning to print'. Perhaps, of all areas of research which the present book draws on, that of research into approaches to the teaching and learning of reading is the most contentious, and therefore the most in need of cool, dispassionate research in order to bring a modicum of sense and balance to the extreme positions often held on this topic. Often the most strident critics of reading standards (and, at times, these have included the British government) have pointed to a move away from 'teaching the basics', by which they often refer to 'phonics': that is to say, sound–letter equivalences in English. But even in the mid-1970s – the period in which the liberalisms of the late 1960s might have been expected to impact – the national survey for the Bullock Committee found that teachers of 6-year-olds were using a range of approaches, with major emphasis on the phonological (i.e. phonetic clusters carrying meaning or significance in the construction of words) and word levels. Of primary teachers, 70 per cent used a phonic approach based on syllables, 97 per cent a phonic approach based on letter sounds, digraphs and diphthongs, 97 per cent used whole word recognition (the 'Look and Say' approach) and 51 per cent used the sentence method. It is immediately obvious from these figures that teachers used more than one method and that the phonological, morphological (grammatical parts of words) and lexical (word) levels were well in use in the teaching of reading during this period. They still are.

The Bullock Report laid much emphasis on the need to understand the *processes* of reading and learning to read as well as the mechanics. In order to define those processes, it proposed three levels of reading skills: the primary, intermediate and advanced. Primary reading skills included the recognition of the shapes of separate letters, groups of letters and whole words, and a working understanding of the grapho-phonemic relationships in English (that is, the first three approaches listed in the previous paragraph). Intermediate skills included the ability to handle sequences of letters, words and larger units of meaning; and the essential reading skills behind such understanding of sequence were anticipation and projection. Reading at each of these levels of size of unit (part of word, word, phrase, sentence, whole text) was characterized by a continual process of anticipating what was coming up and then testing those expectations against what actually came up. Errors of projection might sometimes be genuine attempts to predict the following sequence, using analogy or a stored knowledge of other sequences. Whatever is the case, the Report stresses that phoneme-grapheme relationships are best learnt within the context of actual reading, not in isolation. The point seems obvious, because if learning to read is conceived as the integration of the different levels at which language operates (and which I have set out above), there can be no integration without the different levels being brought together in the learning process. This is why the Report's emphasis on processes rather than the mechanics of reading is essential.

The advanced level of reading skills is termed by the Report that of 'comprehension skills'. These break down into literal comprehension, inferential comprehension, evaluative comprehension and appreciation, the latter taking into account the aesthetic dimension of response. The main point of the Committee's deliberations over literal comprehension was that it was too important a facility to be consigned to multiple-choice exercises or decontextualized passages followed by questions – a common practice in secondary schooling in England and Wales in the 1960s and 1970s. Rather, such literal comprehension 'must be developed in a range of contexts where it is put to a practical purpose, and that means in the various subjects of the curriculum' (p. 121). In the early twenty-first century, in the wake of developments in education that have taken learning beyond the confines of the classroom, we might add to 'various subjects of the curriculum', with its emphasis on language across the curriculum (one of the keynotes of the Report), the following: 'and in the wider world'. The inferential level of text-processing refers to a reading between the lines, and the evaluative to a managing of the range of responses possible from a reading of a text. What is interesting, too, about the appreciative or aesthetic level is that by the end of the twentieth century, it was acknowledged that transactional and functional writing might be as much informed by aesthetic considerations as self-consciously literary works, and that an appreciation of such a dimension – taking into account factors like elegance, harmony, 'unity' and so on – might contribute to the elucidation of the text at every level.

Smith (1999) calls into question the assumption that primary age children can read critically – that is to say, can read at the evaluative and appreciative levels. She cites Hoggart and Freire as examples of those who advocate critical reading: one from the point of view of appreciating texts which have a linguistic and moral complexity, and the other from the perspective of needing, as a reader, to be more powerful than a text in order to be able to see its ideological underpinning. Both positions present the primary teacher with a problem, namely how to inculcate or encourage the process of critical reading in the primary classroom, or how to develop young critical readers. Smith's study, based on ethnographic research with 7- and 8-year-olds, presents accounts of guided reading with the teacher and group reading by the students themselves in collaboration with the researcher. It is clear from the study that the guided classroom reading gives the pupils less space for critical perspective than the group reading session, where their responses are offered and refined in the interactive exchanges within the group. In the latter approach, the text takes on less of a determining presence than in the former; there is therefore more room for inference, evaluation and appreciation, partly because there is more sense of ownership of the text and of the act of reading. Such radically different approaches to developing reading are reflected in the kinds and functions of questions asked. In the former case, the children rarely ask questions, but answer questions set by the teacher as part of the exegesis of the text; in the latter, they pose as well as answer questions, and these are taken up by others in the group and explored more fully. The one-word answer is replaced by a more ruminative exploration of the meaning of the text as construed in the minds of the participants in the group. Although Smith's conclusion is that none of the children she observed in the reading experiments were reading critically (in the evaluative and appreciative senses), they could be said to be understanding that, 'their comments are valued, that reading is a wide-ranging and exploratory practice, and that meaning is personal and interpersonal' (1999: 61). They are, therefore, 'more firmly on the way towards critical reading' (ibid.) than those children who do not have such opportunities.

It is the subject of 'comprehension' or the bringing of meaning to text that is the focus of the next section, which also addresses research on and theories of reader-response.

The act of reading

The act of reading is central to the interpretation of texts, for as Iser (1978) puts it, 'the text represents a potential effect that is realized in the reading process' (p. ix), or, to use an analogy with music and theatre, the score or script is but a mere template for the performance. The music or the play does not exist until the performance makes it happen.

Iser's work is seminal in the development of reader-response theory: a theory that has proved particularly enlightening in the development of practice in the teaching of and appreciation of literary texts. Essentially,

Iser moves the ground of interpretation away from the author and the text, and towards the reader. In its most extreme formulations, reader-response theory operates from the premise that the reader holds all the cards, and that the text is merely a cueing device for the release of those cards in a particular formation (and then, again, in a different formation on a subsequent reading). The ideas that are shaped in Iser's work are not based on empirical research; rather they are shaped *in vacuo* and applied to the reading and interpretation of texts, with examples being provided for illumination. And yet they qualify as research in the sense that the formulation of new ideas, models and approaches qualifies as research.

The reader 'receives' the text, in Iser's thinking, by composing it. That is to say, the act of reading is as creative as the act of composition. Such a conception has implications for both reader and text. For the reader, the act of reading is a constructive, compositional one in which he or she brings not only his/her experience of the world, but also experience of reading other texts. For the text, the embedded affective possibilities are not released until the reader releases them – and then they may not be the same concoction as was released before. 'Thus,' says Iser, 'the meaning of a literary text is not a definable entity but, if anything, a dynamic happening' (1978: 22). It is the *interaction* between reader and text that is the key to the interpretive act.

One of the main objections to reader-response theory is that it is prey to subjectivism and, in the final analysis, can suggest that a text has no meaning other than that of the many subjects who come to it to elicit meanings of their own. Such an objection can be partly answered by arraying reader and text at each end of a spectrum. At one end – that of subjectivism – there is no textual life at all other than the marks on the page or screen. At the other is absolutism, with the text ascribed (by someone!) a single and unarguable meaning. Iser chooses to rid himself of the dualism of the subjective/objective to 'establish an intersubjective frame of reference that will enable us to assess the otherwise ineluctable subjectivity of the value judgements' (1978: 25).

As far as this chapter goes, Iser's thinking provides a raft of varying concepts and approaches that will help us in understanding the nature of advanced skills in reading. Among these are the fact that a reader will go through a number of stages in response to a work: from initial bewilderment as he/she tries to make connection between the words on the page, to layers of interpretation as the words begin to resonate with his/her experience. Later, aesthetic issues come to the fore as the harmony of the whole is considered and the comparison with other works is made. Iser charts the notion of the 'implied reader' that is inherent in all literary texts, whose presence shapes and informs the making of the text. Such a presence is not linguistic, nor able to be analysed by linguistics. Rather, it comes into being as the actual readers make sense of the text in their imaginations, thus bringing the text to life. In summary:

> A reality [the text] that has no existence of its own can only come into being by way of ideation, and so the structure of a text sets off a sequence of mental images which lead to the text translating itself into the reader's consciousness. The actual content of these mental images will be coloured by the reader's existing stock of experience, which acts as a referential background against which the unfamiliar can be conceived and processed. (Iser, 1978: 38)

Examples of the application of Iser's theories to the exploration of responses to fiction and poetry can be found in Protherough (1983) and Benton (2000) respectively.

Surveys of reading difficulties

One of the best collections on reading difficulties is Reid and Donaldson (1977), although the book as a whole uses a diction that now seems part of a deprivation model: terms like 'backwardness', 'retardation' and 'disability' have been replaced in the late twentieth and early twenty-first centuries by a more positive vocabulary. In a chapter on definition and measurement of reading difficulties, Pilliner and Reid (1977) set out the distinction between reading age and chronological age, the difference often being expressed as the 'reading quotient'. They also discuss differences between 'mental age' and 'reading age' according to various intelligence tests, like the Weschler Intelligence Scale for Children and the Stanford-Binet. The aim of such approaches is not so much to aid reading development as to identify those in need of help and to measure progress against standardized norms. As Reid says:

> Firm quantitative evidence about the extent of backwardness and retardation is valuable and even sometimes necessary. It is needed by those who form educational policy, and by those who plan provision. It is needed to inform the public, correct misconceptions and counter complacency. (1977: 37)

In an interesting analysis of reading capabilities in children since the Second World War, Reid cites a number of studies which aimed to gauge the level of reading ability in the school population. Although there has been no consistent application of a single test during this period, she notes that up to the early 1970s, reading standards increased in the English school population from 1948 to 1964 but were no better in 1972 than they were a decade earlier. The proportion of those identified as having reading difficulties varied between 10 per cent and 30 per cent during this period. Because of the nature of large-scale surveys and quantitative normative curves arising from them – and also because of the nature of the definitions employed and the changing nature of literacy, requiring new tests – the proportion of those identified with reading difficulties of a number of kinds remains at about 20 per cent of the population. This figure in itself is not of much use, but it does help to define a group of children and students who need help to attain the basic minimum literacy required by the society at the time.

On an international basis, the International Association for the Evaluation of Educational Achievement conducted 'a survey of reading skills in fifteen countries involving thirteen languages' in 1970–1. Despite difficulties in ensuring comparability, the general result was to identify the gap between 'developed' and 'developing' countries, with an exception being the relatively low standards in reading of US secondary school leavers.

Rutter and Yule (1975) make a distinction between what they call general reading backwardness (again the terminology is that characteristic of the period) which indicates low achievement in reading regardless of intelligence; and specific reading retardation which is low for a child's age with respect to measured IQ. The latter refers 'to a difficulty in learning to read that is not explicable by reference to general intelligence, while in [the former] the reading problem is consistent with relatively poor performance in other areas of ability and attainment' (Pumfrey and Elliott, 1990: 30). There is debate as to the validity and usefulness of this distinction, but there seems to be educational value in the distinction between the two types of children with reading difficulty. For example, in Rutter and Yule's original study, there was a greater proportion of boys with specific reading retardation than with general reading backwardness. Hulme and Snowling (1988) argue that 'the pattern of a child's reading and spelling performance and the way that this changes during development depends upon the interplay of the child's cognitive strengths and weaknesses and methods of tuition' (in Pumfrey and Elliott, 1990: 31). The important point about these and other such studies is that they remind us that difficulties with reading are wider than we sometimes assume – that dyslexia is not necessarily the right diagnosis for some reading problems – and that a number of factors might be at play in any particular case.

All such large-scale surveys of reading capability must be surrounded by caveats. As Reid (1977) points out:

> If surveys of backwardness are based on nothing more than the numerical results of standardized tests, all they can do is to show how the proportion of children scoring below a specified point compares with the proportion in the standardized population. They are therefore useful in showing whether any particular area of the country has a greater or lesser proportion of backward readers than would be expected on the basis of national norms. Observations at intervals over a period of time can show whether there has been a movement in one direction or another and the extent of the change. To find out how bad, in functional terms, the backward children this isolated really are, one has to look at a criterion not in terms of standardized score but in terms of content – how much the children can actually do.

One further significant chapter in Reid and Donaldson's book is that by Little *et al.* (1977), which addresses questions of class size and reading performance in primary schools – a topic that has been a priority in England for the Labour government elected in 1997. They conclude, based on research in England and Scandinavia, that class sizes smaller than 30 in primary schools do not necessarily make for improved reading performance by pupils. Paradoxically, they suggest that such reduction in class size, for all its other benefits, might be linked with lower performance. Two more important factors in ensuring the development and improvement in reading ability in children are the utilization and deployment of staff, with appropriate training and professional development for all staff involved in the teaching of reading; and the influence of social and psychological factors, with support from home being one of the most telling of these.

Readers interested in international perspectives on reading assessment are referred to two linked volumes: Harrison and Salinger (1998) and Coles and Jenkins (1998).

Specific reading difficulties

For much of the 1970s and 1980s, dyslexia was not fully recognized by the education community as a problem which needed early addressing by teachers and others concerned with teaching young children to read.

The Tizard report (Department of Education and Science, 1972), for example, notes that the term 'dyslexia' was 'originally used – and is still applied – by neurologists to describe severe difficulty in reading after a localized injury to the brain of an adult who was previously a competent reader' as well as to children with 'severe reading retardation who had never been competent readers' (quoted in Reid and Donaldson, 1977: 129). Tizard cites the research of Critchley and others who saw dyslexia largely as a neurological dysfunction which, if educational measures designed to overcome reading difficulties fail, may be expected to 'right itself' as the brain matures. Recent and longitudinal studies suggest otherwise. The lack of recognition by educationalists and teachers during the 1970s and 1980s was, it appears, not so much a general refusal to acknowledge dyslexia, as an objection to its use as a blanket term to cover a wide and diverse range of reading difficulties. Without proper definition of the nature of dyslexia, many (supposedly middle-class) parents jumped too quickly to the assumption that difficulties with reading and learning might be attributed to such a label. The spirit of this period is perhaps best caught in this statement from the Tizard report:

> . . . we are highly sceptical of the view that a syndrome of 'developmental dyslexia' with a specific underlying cause and specific symptoms has been identified . . . we think it would be better to adopt a more usefully descriptive term, 'specific reading difficulties', to describe problems of the small group of children whose reading (and perhaps writing, spelling and number) abilities are significantly below the standards which their abilities in other spheres would lead one to expect. (Quoted in Reid and Donaldson, 1977: 131)

One of the most significant recent studies of reading development in dyslexic children is that by Snowling *et al.* (1996), who note the consensus that has emerged concerning the cognitive basis of dyslexia: 'from a developmental perspective, the findings suggest that the underlying cognitive deficit is at the level of phonology' (p. 653).

Although dyslexic children 'may compensate for their reading difficulties [they] often show residual impairments when tested on phonological processing tasks' (ibid.). In order to make results generalizable to a wider population, Snowling *et al.*'s study has taken a sample of 20 dyslexic children from 7 years 7 months to 12 years 7 months. Tentative conclusions are that 'the gradual refinement of phonological representations during development . . . allows the more efficient use of phonology in a range of related tasks, including tests of phonological awareness and verbal short-term memory' (p. 667). The consequence would be that the slowness of dyslexic children's development 'can be conceptualized as a delay in the development of phonological representations' (ibid.).

The most recent edition of Snowling's *Dyslexia* (2000), surveying a plethora of research on the condition in the last fifteen years or so, makes it clear from the outset that dyslexia is a 'life-long, developmental disorder that primarily affects a person's ability to read and spell' and is a 'consequence of a phonological (speech processing) deficit' (p. xiii). The book, 'like the first edition [Snowling, 1987] closes by arguing that individual differences in dyslexia depend on the cognitive strengths that the child brings to the task of learning to read as well as the weaknesses. The behavioural outcome of dyslexia also depends upon the language in which the child is learning and the teaching they receive' (p. xiv).

In practice

As far as reading in the early years is concerned, the Bullock Report's conclusions on the management of the teaching of reading still carry the weight of considerable reflection on the research literature that they carried in the 1970s:

> We . . . consider the best method of organizing reading to be one where the teacher varies the experience between individual, group and class situations according to the purpose in hand. Fundamental to it all is a precise knowledge of the progress and needs of each individual child . . . A particularly important skill is that of assessing the level of difficulty of books by applying measures of readability . . . The effective teacher is one who has under her conscious control all the resources that can fulfil her purpose. By carefully assessing levels of difficulty she can draw from a variety of sources. (p. 113)

In a more recent article, Whitehead (1992) sees the extremes of the 'debate' about literacy to be based on three misconceptions: a failure to understand the nature of literacy; a refusal to face up to the complexity of teaching and learning; and a lack of public language for articulating complex educational issues. The first of these failures manifests itself in a mistaking of the outward show for the real substance of literacy: an obsession with print, with focus on developmental writing without due recognition of the genesis of such practice in psychological explanations of 'early representational thinking in infancy' (p. 4) and a fixed notion that phonics and 'basal readers' are the solution to reading. Particularly telling is her phrase that the 'good old days' of alphabetic and phonic reading instruction 'were the schooldays of the elderly, the middle-aged and the younger adult illiterates who fill community centres and prison literacy classes' (p. 5).

There is still room for further research into the nature of reading, reading development and reading difficulties, and suggestions for these are discussed in the final chapter. Here, I concentrate on implications arising from recent research for the teaching of reading.

It is now well understood by psychologists and reading specialists that learning to read is a complex activity. It involves gaining command of levels of language, ranging from small units to larger ones, and also integrating those levels in the bringing of meaning to text. Although there has been much research on the different levels, with most of it being concentrated on the smaller units (the grapho-phonemic and morphological levels), less is known about the integration of the various levels at which language operates. In the light of the current state of knowledge, the implications for practitioners in helping children to learn to read are that:

- learning to read is not simply a matter of decoding print; it is a symbiotic process in which decoding print and 'bringing meaning to text' work in tandem to develop reading capacity;
- knowledge of each of the levels at which language can be described is important for reading teachers;
- deployment of the appropriate levels at which to reinforce or develop knowledge will be a matter of judgement for the teacher in relation to the particular stage of development of the child, or the particular difficulties he or she is encountering;

- teachers undertaking their own case studies of children reading will be a valuable addition to the research literature, but also will provide insights for the teacher into the needs of the particular cases and the more general issues in learning to read;
- paired and shared reading is a valuable asset in the range of pedagogical approaches needed in a school's reading programme;
- home–school liaison is critical in reading development;
- a supply of continually updated fiction and non-fiction is essential to inspire young readers;
- reading on-screen, from CD-ROMs, online from other sources is an art in itself. Young people should be encouraged to be active readers of electronic text, reshaping, repurposing, downloading and editing to suit their particular needs;
- with regard to dyslexia, reinforcement of the grapho-phonemic relations in English needs to be established as soon as the problem is identified;
- visual cues in learning to read are to be explored and valued.

Note

1   The Bullock Report built much of its commentary on language education on a large-scale survey of primary and secondary schools. Two questionnaires were completed in January 1973 by a random sample of 1,415 primary and 392 secondary schools. Written evidence was invited from 66 individuals and 56 organizations, with many more offering further evidence from personal experience, published and original research.

Chapter 5

Teaching Literature

This chapter is not so much about the teaching of particular literary texts, but about the teaching of literature in general and the research that can inform it. Whereas Chapter 4 focused on the teaching of reading at the sentence level and below, this chapter focuses more on the interpretation and appreciation of whole (largely fictional) texts. The two dimensions of reading are closely interrelated.

We should start with a fundamentally important book for all teachers of literature: Thomas Pavel's *Fictional Worlds* (1986). This book suggests that fictions are but one kind of 'possible world'. The notion of possible worlds runs back to modal logic philosophy of the early 1970s, and further back to philosophical and literary speculations about other worlds and their significance. What Pavel is saying, essentially, is that print-located fictions are worlds that have boundaries and which themselves are located in relation to the supposed real world.

It is important to establish the nature of fiction at the outset, because all too often readers (students and teachers alike) assume that novels, plays and even poems are depictions of the real world. These readers therefore bring to the fictions a naïve belief that the characters in the fiction are 'real' and abide by the same laws and *mores* of the world inhabited by the reader. At one extreme, such a transparent, innocent reading of fiction is delightful, with its immersion and suspension of disbelief marking part of the pleasure of reading fiction; but at this same extreme, pathological identification with a character can lead to or be a result of personality disorder.

Reader response

Perhaps the other major source for thinking about the teaching of literature over the last twenty to thirty years has been Wolfgang Iser's book, *The Act of Reading: a theory of aesthetic response* (1978), already discussed in Chapter 4.

The privileging of the reader in the act of reading is a humanist, teacherly position to take. It enables the exploration of a number of approaches to the reading of a text and due recognition of the role that readers play in the creation of meaning. Most significantly, emphasis upon the reader allows for pedagogical invention in that it opens up the possibility of multiple meanings mediated by readers. The business of teaching a book becomes not so much a matter of exegesis or leading one's students to 'appreciate' the qualities of a work, but enabling access to it and allowing the readers to make their own versions of it.

Reader-response theory has therefore aligned itself with directed activities relating to texts (DARTS), the more creative and open-ended devices for dealing with fictional works. These have provided a more enjoyable and usually more illuminating approach to textual analysis than comprehension exercises which conventionally take an excerpt from a work and set a number of questions on it, ranging from the simply literal to the more complexly interpretive. Just as was discussed earlier in the book, in Chapter 2 in relation to the use of questions in classrooms, so too literature teaching has moved beyond the question as a device for eliciting response.

One criticism which could be levelled against reader-response approaches to the teaching of literature is that by giving disproportionate space to readers, they miss the subtleties embodied in the text. Such readings are not so much a problem of the approach itself, but rather of a poor application of the approach. Another criticism is that reader-response advocates are driven by a humanist paradigm that looks back to a Leavisite attitude which erects 'good literature' as the keystone of English curricula. In the face of postmodernism, 'exploding English' and the ICT revolution, literature looks like a safe haven. Interestingly, there has been little research into reader response to non-fictional texts.

For a full account of the history of reader-response research, see Squire (1990). His comprehensive review of research, dating back to the work of I. A. Richards in the 1920s, concludes that:

- the teaching of literature must focus on the transaction between the reader and the work;
- response is affected by prior knowledge and prior experience;
- response is affected by prior knowledge and prior experience and it differs with time and place;
- response to literature varies with rhetorical mode (e.g. narrative and non-narrative types of text);
- large numbers of readers generally share a common response to a particular literary text, yet no two responses are alike;
- works of genuine literary quality can evoke a richer, more meaningful experience than those that I. A. Richards calls 'pseudo-literature';
- it takes two to read a book, i.e. 'much of the value of the reading experience comes from thinking about, or talking about, or writing about the work' (p. 20);
- important developmental differences can be seen in the ways children respond to literature;
- the sounds of words are often as important as the sense;
- the ways in which we teach literature will affect our students' responses.

As Squire (1990) goes on to say: 'these ten principles . . . should form the basic strategies for redirecting the attention of teachers and students to literature-centred teaching. From all that we have learned about the response of the reader, these seem to be the most important' (p. 22). At the same time, there is always the need for further research. Again, the following points could not be clearer:

- we need greater insight into the ways in which response develops during the complete process of reading literature;
- considered study must explore concretely the ways in which programmes for teaching reading comprehension and programmes for developing response to literature can best be integrated . . . in the classroom;
- we need clearer guidelines on how literary appreciation or mature responses develop over a period of time;
- we need to bring together, in ways more useful for teachers and teaching, what we know from research in cognitive development and the teaching of comprehension about the impact of schema

and prior knowledge on reading, with the insights from literary theories of various persuasions.

To add to this summary list, Turner (1996) suggests that it is further understanding of the processes we engage in the act of reading, rather than after the act, that are the most important to explore. To demonstrate a relatively unexplored aspect of reading, he analyses his own responses to a short story. The aim of the exercise is to move classroom practice away from 'the sterile lit. crit. essay [and] the ubiquitous book review' (p. 34) towards responses that are sensitive to the key moments of response and learning during the reading of a book.

Framing and interpretation

In the next chapter I refer to the work of McLachlan and Reid (1994) on the framing of still and moving images in relation to verbal framing. Here, my concern is with the central thrust of McLachlan and Reid's book, which is directed at the framing and interpretation of discourse and literature. They argue that even in the interpretation of short narratives that occur in everyday conversational exchanges, 'acts of *extratextual framing* are always involved – "extratextual" in the sense that they depend on seemingly "outside" (*extra*) information, unspecified by the text but felt to be presupposed by it' (p. 3). McLachlan and Reid also define *intratextual* frames (the way in which the flow of words within the text is affected by subdivisional or other internal framing devices), *intertextual* frames (the ways texts or text-types relate to each other) and *circumtextual* features like the presence of references, nature of title, bibliography and index in a book of this kind. The acts of framing are the focus of the McLachlan and Reid book, rather than the frames themselves, which are often intangible, sub-liminal – and even if they are material – prone to erasure in the eye of the beholder.

There is a clear connection between framing and reader-response approaches to the interpretation of literature in that reader-response theories presuppose the reader is bringing something to the act of reading text on a page. Among other predispositions, readers bring experience of the world, an emotional inscription, knowledge of other texts, the contingencies of the particular moment (mood, inclination, whether they are alone or in a particular group, etc.). Each of these sets of assumptions can be characterized as 'frames' and their particular configuration in relation to an act of reading will influence the actual experience. Furthermore, not only will the individual reader bring a different set of frames to a particular reading each time he or she encounters the text; other individuals will bring their own sets of frames to the same text. Interpretations will therefore differ, although there may be some consensus. That consensus may well be more to do with the nature of the group than the nature of the text.

From a more practical perspective, Martin and Leather (1994) explore what happens in 'reading moments' for readers in the primary years. Their basic tenet is that 'what happens when we read is basically the same regardless of age. Indeed the same process appears to be at work when very young children are read stories in the pre-school years' (p. 5). The difficulty of tracing developmental stages in reading from such a perspective is described by Appleyard (1990). Such suggestions of a universal set of stages do not

> . . . capture the gradual, incremental and multifaceted process by which development occurs in particular readers as they traverse a lifetime of stories, poetry and dramas. Nor can they take account of personal history, intelligence, personality traits, and unique likes and dislikes, which . . . may explain what is most distinctive about how a particular person reads. Neither can a schematic description of the main lines of development take more than a partial account of factors such as gender, race, class and economic level by which the experience of large groups of readers is socially mediated. (Quoted in Martin and Leather, 1994: 5–6)

Martin and Leather's book contains a very useful chapter on implications of a reader-response approach for the primary classroom.

The centrality of literature?

West (1994), in a chapter entitled 'The Centrality of Literature', affirms the proposition that 'literature is, and should remain, central to the teaching and learning of English in the secondary curriculum' (p. 124), but notes that this 'seemingly widespread agreement . . . is deceptively reassuring and disguises substantial ideological differences' (ibid.). West's chapter sheds much light on the question of models of English discussed earlier in this book (see Chapter 1). His own position is that we need to 'start with texts rather than with literature', which 'brings us back to critical literacy' (p. 129). It is worth quoting at length:

> English in the version proposed here takes a more investigative and analytical approach to the whole question of literature. It assumes the existence of literatures and canons and questions what it is about particular texts that has led particular groups to privilege them in this way. The point is not to contest one particular canon and seek to replace it with another: that way lies endless sterile contention. Nor does it seek to impose adherence to any one selection. Students must be free to make their own cultural and literary affiliations; our responsibility is to help them to a greater understanding of the implications of their own and others' choices. They need opportunities to see texts in their full social contexts and histories, to understand the assumptions underlying both the texts and the valuations put on them by particular groups. (Ibid.)

The question of critical literacy is explored in Morgan (1997). There are key principles to a critical literacy approach (or approaches) to the study of literature. Among these are the refusal to see a dichotomy between theory and practice, a commitment to seeing texts in their political contexts, a resistance to 'certain' or hegemonic readings, a consideration of the pleasure of texts, an understanding of the dialogic and situated nature of discourse and, above all, the celebration of a critical spirit in the social practice of teaching and learning literature.

In a small-scale study of teacher attitudes towards the teaching of English, Beavis (1995) interviewed nine teachers about their experience of teaching texts in senior English and literature classrooms. In their recommendations, teachers 'stressed detailed knowledge of texts, the centrality of individual experiences as a reader, and the need for a rich and diverse range of classroom strategies' (p. 25), with further directions being suggested which included understanding the role of the English teacher in a school culture, and of the school culture within a wider societal culture; the place of literature in relation to media texts; and the importance of understanding that practice in literature classrooms is based on theories and ideologies that need unpacking. If anything, a key move forward would be applications of theory to practice so that both advanced and reluctant readers might benefit.

Gender differences

Swann (1992) was cited earlier in this book with regard to differences in the ways that boys and girls were perceived to speak and listen; there are differences, too, as far as choice of reading is concerned. Her summary findings are that there are more male characters than female in children's stories, textbooks and other non-fiction; and more male authors of literary texts studied by older pupils. Males and females are often presented in fiction in stereotyped ways. Despite the fact that several studies in the early 1970s pointed out the gender imbalance and despite the fact of increased positive representation of girls and women in fiction and textbooks, there was still in 1990 an imbalance – a bias in favour of male representation in diverse roles. Nevertheless, girls performed better than boys, on average, in tests of reading and writing at both 11 and 16; girls tend to enjoy school-related reading and writing activities; girls' reading preferences are more akin to the school's perceptions of what a reading curriculum should be – so that non-fiction, special interest magazines and computer games are less likely to form part of the school library than fiction. The extent to which a school builds its English curriculum on fiction may well determine the extent to which boys see English as a subject to enjoy – or not. As always, there are qualifications and caveats to be made:

> Differences in girls' and boys' aptitudes and choices may be related to several factors . . . perceptions of school reading and writing as 'quiet' and 'passive' activities, which may make them appeal more to girls than to boys; the lack of appeal of many school reading books for boys; girls' relative lack of confidence in their academic abilities and their perceptions of English as an undemanding subject. (Swann, 1992: 134)

Literature and the other arts

A central tenet in arguments for the centrality of literature in English has been that literature is an art. A more radical position takes all language work to be an art, but here we are talking about degrees of aestheticism. Let us take, for the moment, the proposition that literature (i.e. fictional works) is analogous to dance, drama, art and music – often referred to collectively as 'the arts'. Rather than discuss the arguments for this position (see, for example, Abbs, 1976, 1982, 1987), let us concentrate on research into the teaching of literature.

One of the proponents of such work is Benton (Benton, 1984; Benton and Fox, 1985; Benton *et al.*, 1988; Benton, 2000). In *Young Readers Responding to Poems* (Benton *et al.*, 1988), a number of small-scale research studies are described which look at students' responses and the teaching methods employed to bring them about (or indeed prevent them occurring!). In the book, Teasey describes a study in which five readers were asked to compile an anthology of 20 of their favourite poems: half of the poems were to be agreed upon and the other half were to be individual choices. Research took the form of the students recording the processes they went through in selecting, justifying and organizing their anthology. It was thus a project that at the same time as eliciting research results about the nature of reading also provided an enjoyable and focused teaching and learning experience. As with much of the research cited in this book, readers will have to go to the source to get a full account of the work undertaken. The essential points are that there is a paradox at the heart of the process of reading fictional works: 'in the interaction between reader and text, the reader attends twice, to the world of the text, and to the world within him, generated by the text' (Benton *et al.*, 1988: 64). In Rosenblatt's terms, the poem acts both as a stimulus and as a blueprint for the act of reading and interaction. Reading poems becomes a wave-like activity, with successive readings washing over the text, each wave bringing more to the reading and carrying the residue not only of previous experience ('real' and literary) but of earlier readings. Each reading may have a different function. Teasey asks some important questions which are partly answered by his study, but which require further research:

1. What is the significance of the first response?
2. What is the significance of the first unbroken series of responses?
3. What has been achieved by this initial response and/or series of responses?
4. What is the significance of the subsequent re-entry point?
5. What is the significance of subsequent re-readings?
6. What has been achieved by the time the reader closes the process of responding privately?
7. What is the significance of the follow-up?

Such intensive reading practices are most suited to short texts, like poems. When larger texts, like novels or plays, are encountered, the same questions apply but the process might be compressed somewhat. While we all subscribe to the fact that a first reading of a novel or short story is different from a second – largely because in the first reading we do not know what is coming next – the pedagogies differ from those used in the reading of poems. The first reading of a largely narrative work is predicated on projection of what is to come, and the actual reading of text is confirmed by or is surprised by what actually comes. The balance or mismatch between expectation and actuality is part of the pleasure of that kind of text. In subsequent readings, the process is more like revisiting a site where one already knows its parameters: the attention is more on the structure, the language used to evoke the responses, the texture of the work. In other words, it is more on the spatial qualities of the work and less on the narrative drive. Sensitivity to these different kinds of reading is essential to the enjoyable and effective teaching of literature.

Benton (2000) is the result of twenty years or so of work at the interface of the verbal and visual – or, more specifically, on the pedagogical possibilities in the relations between poems and works of art. The book, however, is no mere pedagogical guide. It is a thorough investigation of the territory between poems and art works.

The opening chapters set out the theory behind the space, as it were, between the reader/looker and the poem/work of art. Although the book is entitled *Studies in the* Spectator *Role*, it would be more accurately described as studies in participant/spectator roles, as one of its central tenets is that the spectator role, as described by Britton and others, always implies participation of some kind. To some, such reciprocity between spectator and participant is paradoxical; to others, contradictory. This particular issue is a matter of where you stand in relation to the human condition. Putting aside philosophical paralysis of this kind, Benton attempts to chart the spectrum of positions on the participant/spectator axis, concluding that each end of the spectrum contains degrees of the other.

That position is limiting for the book as a whole; culturally, the sensibility is one informed by the collection of the Tate Gallery of British Art. The paintings and sculptures cited are by Millais, Turner, Unton, Hogarth, Blake, Wilson, Constable, Spencer, Gormley and others: almost all men and certainly all British (mostly English). One could argue that the combination of cultural narrowness, aesthetic distance and an over-dependence on reader-response theories renders the whole enterprise nostalgic rather than illuminating; but not so, for the book has a commitment and rigour of analysis that makes it well worth a close read. As the author himself admits, the book's purposes are not to address these wider agendas, but to 'provide a rationale for the complementary study of these two art forms, with particular reference to painting in Britain and with the National Curriculum [for England] requirements to teach pre-twentieth century literature in mind' (Benton, 2000: 6).

The exposition of Rosenblatt-derived thinking on the nature of reader response is one of the best summaries of its kind, with an acknowledgement that one problem reader response has left unresolved is the complexity of the role of the reader as a virtual construct. There is insightful analysis of the role of key thinkers like Britton, Iser, Walton and others to the debate. References to Pavel's 1986 book, *Fictional Worlds*, are minimal and further exploration of the concepts of distance and boundaries to fictional worlds would have added to the discussion; but one of Benton's points is that the metaphorical notion of 'worlds' as applied to the experience of reading fiction is itself in need of critique. The collective point of the three opening chapters is summed up in a quotation from Lamarque and Olsen's philosophical *Truth, Fiction and Literature*: 'the twin perspectives of imaginative involvement and awareness of artifice are both indispensable in an appropriate response to works of fiction' (p. 25). To 'attend twice at once' is at the heart of the reader/viewer as maker paradox.

The problem with poetry

I based the book, *The Problem with Poetry* (Andrews, 1991), on action research work with students and teachers in Hong Kong, New York, London and York over a 15-year period. Poetry presents particular problems for teachers and students alike in that it is not widely read and – like Shakespeare – comes at the bottom of young people's preferences in reading literature; the language or diction of poetry is often seemingly impenetrable; the range of poems studied is often narrow; it is taught in conventional ways that presuppose the purpose of teaching it is to elucidate 'difficult' language and for students to gain appreciation of 'high culture'; and it is often reduced to a hunt for similes and metaphors, as if they were the *sine qua non* of poetry (when in fact they are features of many different types of language). Teachers' attitudes to it are crucial.

The central formal problem in giving access to poetry was seen to be understanding and appreciating the way rhythm worked in a poem. The lack of a prosody for free verse, in particular, highlighted the difficulty in talking about the operation of rhythm in many of the poems encountered by young people in school anthologies. Solutions were found in extending the range of poems read in class, beyond those informed by the ideology of 'emotion recollected in tranquility' and cast in the conventional forms of verses, stanzas and regular metres. Such an extension of the range required an international approach to uncover poems in diverse forms, using more than one voice, in different rhythms and with political edge.

The first act of the teacher concerned with enhancing the poetic experience of his or her students, then, is the seeking out of exciting and appropriate poems that will open up students' sense of what is possible in verse, make clear distinctions between it and prose, and enable the writing of poems by students that will establish them as writers in their own right alongside published writers. In these and other ways, the aim of the reported research is to break down barriers between students and poetry by opening them up to the diversity of international practice.

Global perspectives

Two books from the USA stake out a claim to approach literature from a wider – indeed, global – perspective. They are Lott *et al.* (1993) and Trimmer and Warnock (1992). Most of the essays in these edited collections are 'comparatist': that is to say they use comparative method-ologies to weigh up the characteristics of particular texts. The ideological drive is pluralist, with a 'need for the expansion of literature programs to include a wider range of cultures and nationalities' (p. 1). The advantages of such an eclectic canon are not only that the curriculum is internationalist and an awareness of the variety of human experience is cultivated; but also, and perhaps in research terms, more acutely, 'it initiates a developmental "othering" process that clarifies values because it obliges readers to match their own frameworks against different systems of reality' (p. 15). One could argue that literature *per se* fulfils this latter function because of its invitation to explore possible worlds, as we have seen above in the discussion of Pavel and others. But reading literature from other countries and cultures can extend the imaginative leap that students have to make and thus help them to achieve more in terms of their own sensibilities and imaginative development.

Another aspect of a global dimension to teaching literature arises from the nature of the literature itself. Following Bakhtin (1981), Hawkins (1993), in a bibliographic essay, discusses intertextuality and cultural identity. She argues that identity for readers of all ages is partly affected by the books they encounter, and that the books themselves are part of conversations that have been influenced by existing literature and cultural histories. Works that interleave, as it were, echoes of other works and (by implication) other cultures, other voices – these represent the hybrid nature of contemporary identities. In other words, diversity, boundary crossing, displacement and hybridity are more common than supposedly monocultural conceptions of literary and cultural history and (therefore) identity. To talk about 'English Literature', then, is to confine oneself unnecessarily to a figment of the imagination rather than to any identifiable nexus of characteristics. As Dasenbrock (1992: 45) puts it:

> All interpersonal communication involves translation and interpretation. We are never in complete command of the language produced by others, yet to live is to come to an understanding of others. Theories suggesting that we never manage to do so are both inaccurate and are likely to confirm us in the prison of our own narrow cultural horizons.

A curriculum development and research project undertaken by McGuinn, Andrews and Hakes (1993) involved postgraduate teaching students and students from two 16–19 colleges in Hull, England. The aim was to introduce literary texts from other cultures than a narrowly conceived English one, and then to work out teaching strategies for work with the recipient students in the colleges. One of the striking results of the research was that the postgraduate teacher trainees found the discovery of 'international' texts a revelation in itself. Many had not read outside the confines of the narrow English tradition, and most were unaware of the Anglocentric nature of their diet to date. Even works by Scottish, Welsh or Irish writers were somehow subsumed within English literature by the sleight of hand (or historical accident) that conflated the English language with the island on which it was fashioned.

One of the aims of the project was to widen the literary horizons against – at the time – government proposals to narrow the canon of books read in school. These horizons included not only the geographical, but also an attempt to include more women writers in the canon: Atwood, Shange, Allende, Jhabvala, Tan and Ratushinakaya, among others. Achievements of the project, as evaluated, were its success in introducing sixth-form students, university Postgraduate Certificate in Education students and their teachers and lecturers to a wider range of literature than that to which they had been previously exposed; the broadening of literary sensibilities at a time when the National Curriculum in England and Wales was trying to narrow the literary canon used in schools and colleges; the nature of the subject 'English' was expanded for those involved, who also questioned their previous notions of 'Englishness' and the question of translation into English.

Other key articles from differing national and cultural perspectives include Naidoo (1995), Anderson (1995), Chandran (1995), Bryan (1995) and Ali (1995). Naidoo writes of her own experiences of racism in South Africa as well as in England, affirming that part of understanding what a reader brings to a text must take into account the politics of their upbringing and experiences as well as those of the writer and the text: 'in order to begin to understand racism, young people need to have some historical knowledge. They need to begin to grasp how racism is communicated and how language is central to that communication. They need to understand how their own identities have been shaped and that they are capable of reshaping aspects of themselves' (Naidoo, 1995: 12). Literature can play its part in this reshaping, but it has to be literature that is carefully chosen and carefully taught so as not to reconfirm prejudices. Identity is also an issue for Anderson (1995), who gives an account of the development of the Norwegian national curriculum, recognizing as it does the links between types of national language and identity.

Chandran (1995) draws on the literature of framing to propose that reading frames – the borrowing of one construct in order to understand or shed light on another – can help in the appreciation of a difficult poem like 'The Waste Land'. In so doing, he suggests that one of the most exciting aspects of teaching English can be the connections students make between one work and another, thus realizing Bakhtin's notion of intertextuality. 'The Waste Land' is a particularly appropriate text with which to experiment, but the principle can be applied to a range of texts and at various stages of education. Bryan (1995) analyses responses to Caribbean poetry in Jamaica and in England, concluding that the different contexts lend a good deal to the reading of the poems – and that each brings its own particular qualities to bear on the reading. Lastly, in the collection of articles in *English in Education*, Ali (1995) examines the teaching of literature in a Malaysian second language-learning context, revealing not only the possibilities evident with a new curriculum and an open-minded attitude towards construing texts, but wider issues about the teaching of literature to students of English as a second language, and the cultural baggage – or lack of it – that accompanies the interpretive act.

One of the best collections of papers on bilingualism as it pertains to the teaching of literature is *Reading Against Racism* (Evans, 1992), in which writers from cultures around the world reflect on their particular circumstances to shed light on literary practices in the classroom in the UK. The spirit of the book is captured in Salman Rushdie's (1990) statement: 'Human beings understand themselves and shape their futures by arguing and challenging and questioning the unsayable; not by bowing the knee, whether to gods or men.' *Reading Against Racism* therefore assumes literary texts are propositions to be argued with rather than sacred texts. From a book in which all the chapters are worth reading, I will select two for particular mention: those by Denise Newfield about reading against racism in South Africa, and by Sibani Raychaudhuri about English and Bengali verse. Others chapters focus on the situation in the USA, Australia, Finland and the UK.

Newfield's (1992) chapter reminds us of the political context in which literature takes its place. Reading is never a politically neutral activity, and in South Africa in the late 1980s and early 1990s the political situation was especially foregrounded in reading practices. Newfield warns that reading alone will not remove racism from the system, but rather 'the eradication of racism in education in South Africa depends on the eradication of racism in social, economic and political spheres' (p. 40). However, this does not mean that teachers must not play a part in the changing of a racist system by introducing and developing syllabi that actively promote a tolerant, wide sensibility as far as the selection of texts is concerned. Ironically, the set texts in the 1980s and early 1990s in South Africa were in the Eurocentric tradition. Newfield quotes Janks and Paton (1991):

> The reason for this decision is obvious. Much of the literature published in recent times by both black and white writers has been

'political'. Authors have portrayed again and again the hardships and injustices suffered by South Africans under the apartheid system. Three taboo subjects in South African schools are sex, politics and religion, and literature which deals explicitly with these topics is considered suspect. The study of elitist British high culture protects us from having to focus on the terrifying problems of the world in which we live. (p. 227)

Newfield proposes a range of approaches for combating racism through reading: critical or oppositional reading of overtly or covertly racist texts; reading of texts that are in themselves anti-racist; and the promotion of reading skills through texts that reconstruct in literature a new present. These reading skills have elsewhere been called 'critical reading skills' in that they equip readers to get behind the surface of texts to explore and critique the ideologies underpinning them.

Raychaudhuri (1992) gives an account of action research in classrooms of 12–13-year-olds where she introduces poems by Auden and Tagore, in English and Bengali, to young people from a range of cultural backgrounds. The aim of introducing poems in familiar and unfamiliar languages is to give students experience of what it is like to embrace a new language and culture; to give some introductory experience of translation; to become aware of the extent to which languages borrow words from one another; and to gauge the similarities as well as the differences between the two poems in question.

The assessment of reading development

Although research into the ability to decode is extensive (see Chapter 3), there is little on the assessment of development in reading at the higher interpretive levels: that is to say, at the levels of the paragraph or section of text, the text as a whole and the contexts in which reading takes place. Millard (1994) notes that 'few schools can provide a detailed overview of their pupils' performance' (p. 173). Quoting a Nottingham-shire study, she suggests that few schools reported using any systematic approaches to monitoring the effectiveness of teaching reading and most schools were unable to provide evidence of trends in reading achieve-ment. At best, records account for the number of books read and the range of reading, rather than cognitive advances or descriptions of increasing sensitivity in the act of reading. Certainly one-off tests are no indication of the quality or depth of a student's reading, and the best hope is to continue to work to devise 'kinds of information that teachers and pupils can collect over time in order to create a comprehensive picture of individual achievement' (p. 174).

One of the best kinds of information has taken the form in the last ten to fifteen years of portfolios of reflections on reading. As Millard suggests, such a portfolio might include teachers' logs of observations in different contexts; systematic records of pupil–teacher reading conferences; samples of passages selected for reading aloud; a comment book shared by teacher, pupil and parent or guardian; children's own records of the books they have read; and children's reviews of particular genres. To this list can be added writing generated by reading; records of documentary material gathered from books or the Internet; and anthologies created by the students themselves. One particular assignment that is rarely used is an account by the student of his or her 'reading history', somewhat like a reading autobiography which focuses not only on the books read, but on the processes of reflection experienced in the acts of reading.

As we noted in the chapter on reading, national tests of reading ability are notoriously simplistic, given that the business of reading is a complex network of capabilities. Often comprehension tests or exercises, or tests in which a number of facets of reading ability are distilled into a single mark or grade, give no indication of the breadth of reading skill – nor, indeed, any indication of where weaknesses might lie. One of the key conclusions that Millard reaches in the light of her research is that 'sampling populations at regular intervals by a range of reading tasks is a more effective way of monitoring reading standards than is provided by assessment procedures' (1994: 187) linked to national curricula.

Protherough (1993) asks what has been learnt from research into A level [Advanced level] literature teaching and examining and sets four questions that demand clear answers: 'What is it that counts as learning (and as success) in literature that we propose to measure? For whom and for what purposes is that measuring attempted? What range of measurements is available to us? What is it that we do not or cannot currently measure?' (p. 11).

In answer to the first question, Protherough suggests that knowledge, understanding, technical skills and responsiveness are the 'potentially measurable' qualities in literary competence, but notes that at different periods (and indeed by different examination boards), different emphases have been put on one or another of these four qualities. To the second question, he records that literature can be used in these different ways:

- evaluatively, to show how successfully learning has gone on;
- diagnostically, to show students' strengths and weaknesses;
- comparatively, to show how students have performed in relation to
    their own past record
    others in the group
    national norms
    some abstract 'ideal' standard;
- predictively, to forecast future success, or as a selection tool. (Protherough, 1993: 14)

In terms of measurements available to gauge response to literature, Protherough identifies a range from the open and impressionistic at one end of the spectrum to the more controlled and formal at the other. Under 'observation and interpretation' come the interpretation of individuals' reading habits and the evaluation of participation; under 'manipulating the reading process or the text' come controlling the act of reading to provide an indicator of response and manipulating texts to provide potential indicators of response; and typical of 'controlling or restricting response' are teacher-directed responses and formal, extended written responses.

Finally, what are the qualities that English teachers wish to develop but which are often ignored by formal assessment? First there 'are no "scientific" measures to discover how much pleasure and satisfaction students are gaining from their literature courses [and] how they use the reading abilities they are developing' (p. 17). Second, 'if assessment is taken to mean those "simple pencil-and-paper tests" or formal examinations beloved by some theorists, then it is clear that we can learn little or nothing from them about such vital issues as the kind of development shown by an individual over a period of time, or the ability to participate in and to learn from group discussions of a text' (ibid.). Third, 'testing does not account for re-reading, the continuing process through which students modify their realization of texts' (ibid.). Readers interested in these and related issues are recommended to read Protherough (1986).

In a report produced for schools in Suffolk, England, Daw (1996) examined six schools in the county which regularly did well in the proportion of high grades attained in English Literature syllabuses at Advanced level (exams taken usually at 18). Methods used included lesson observation, interview and the analysis of written work. What the investigation found was that a number of factors affected the performance of students, with the chief among them being the following:

- well-qualified and informed specialist staff;
- teachers who retain a strong enthusiasm for literature and are active readers of contemporary literature, writers, theatre-goers and critics themselves;
- teachers who see the intellectual development of students as their primary concern;
- careful selection and pairing of staff, so that experience and innovation are balanced;
- balanced teaching approaches which enable exposition, exegesis and exploration to take place;
- ways are found of building a sense of the relationship between texts;
- providing students with models of high-quality critical discussion;
- high-quality marking and feedback in ways that promote development and communicate high expectations.

The implications for programme development were clear: teachers needed in-service training which focused as much on the exploration of new reading as on pedagogical techniques; and differentiation of approaches, with a strong consideration of development over the period of a course, were essential elements in planning. For students, the key attribute was wider reading both before and during a programme.

Implications for practice

The last thirty years have seen a considerable amount of research devoted to the nature and practices of reading fiction. This research has drawn on psychology, sociology, cultural studies and other disciplines as well as on English and education. Perhaps the key advances are that we now know much more about the processes and acts of reading; we are more informed about global perspectives on reading and more aware of the culturally selective nature of canons; and we have continued to think about the teaching of literature in relation to the other arts.

The implications for practice that arise from such research are:

- further understanding is needed that fictional works are framed cultural artefacts, operating within a rhetorical space that is quite distinctive: the reader brings expectations to it; attitudes to it are shaped by the book;
- we need a more balanced attitude towards the place of fiction in relation to television programmes, film, video, theatre and other cultural forms;
- the process of reading – with anticipation, projection, reorientation, etc. – needs to be understood and applied to the teaching of literature;
- variation needs to be built into the teaching of the 'class reader' so that readers of all abilities will benefit from the activity of reading a book in a large group;
- teachers need to be enthusiastic readers of contemporary fiction to maintain the tradition of literature as a living cultural force;
- young people should continue to be encouraged to read widely, and to make connections between all aspects of their reading (and viewing).

Chapter 6

Viewing Still and Moving Images

There is a small but growing amount of research into 'viewing' in relation to language development. This chapter divides itself between addressing the research into the relation of still images and words on the one hand, and moving images and language development on the other. It is the latter field that has seen most curriculum development in the last thirty or so years, but the former which needs to be addressed first, because in order to understand the function of the *moving* image in education, we must first understand the nature and function of the still image in relation to verbal language. In this and the next chapter I draw on my own research and that of those with whom I have been closely associated. There is much to argue for in relation to the roles of the visual and ICT in relation to English teaching – indeed, a new conception of the curriculum field, based on multimedia, may well subsume what we have taken to be 'English' (i.e. a text-based discipline) over the past eighty years or so.

Visual literacy

Much of the key recent research has been Arts Council funded. This is because the Arts Council has recognized that in the wake of semiotics the arts are often seen in terms of a *language* – a shorthand for a 'semiotic system'. There is much resistance in the visual arts world, in particular, to such a formulation; but also an acknowledgement that it is hard to place the visual arts in society without using verbal language. One of the key pieces of research in the area in the last few years has been Raney (1997).

In *Visual Literacy: Issues and Debates* she sets out the problems of the term 'visual literacy', noting that 'literacy' as a term has tended to be appended to a range of forms of communication, like 'emotional literacy', 'cultural literacy' and even 'soccer literacy'. Visual literacy itself has been used, on the whole, to denote a cluster of vision capabilities rather than to give too much emphasis to the 'literacy' side of the coupling. This has meant that the effort has been to map the capabilities (in earlier less sophisticated versions, 'skills' or 'competences') of the visual, linking them to assumptions, beliefs and expectations. One of the most useful definitions of the term comes from Messaris (1994), who uses the term to mean 'greater experience with the workings of visual media coupled with a heightened conscious awareness of those workings' (p. 2). Raney goes on to set out the four consequences said to flow from such a definition of visual literacy: comprehension of visual media, transfer of cognitive skills from the intepretations of visual media to other tasks, awareness of visual manipulation and aesthetic appreciation (1997: 15).

The beginnings of a visual vocabulary are set out in a section entitled 'Visual Language'. As Raney points out (p. 47), each of the different senses in which visual language is used draws upon a particular dimension of the meaning of 'language':

1. *The visual has communicative potential.* The first, broadest sense in which the visual is said to be or have a language is by virtue of the fact that visual objects or images can communicate. Denying the visual a language would seem to deny it communicative potential . . . Thus one speaks loosely of the language of music, the language of bees, the language of emotions, the language of gestures and so on.

2. *Visual objects and images have parts which are arranged in certain relationships. The nature of the parts and the relationships between them affects what is communicated.* In this more developed version, which often follows on from the first, an analogy is made between constituent elements found in visual products and the elements of sentences, paragraphs and verbal texts. Then an analogy is made between the arrangement of these elements and the 'syntax' and 'grammar' of verbal language.

3. *The visual products made by an individual are usually consistent in terms of how that individual's concerns are*

articulated through particular materials. This consistency is felt to amount to a kind of personal language. This sense of visual language is close to notions of style, but using the word 'language' suggests a repertoire of symbols, marks, colours, subjects, ways of working which can be called upon in a particular instance of making, much as an individual's vocabulary can be called upon in a moment of speech. Put in Saussurean terms, an artist can be said to develop an individual 'langue' in which each work will be an instance – 'parole' – of this.

This third sense moves the visual away from verbal language, though inescapably using words to express its position and relation to the rest of the world of discourse. There are more senses in which the visual can be described in terms of language (Raney, 1997: 47–8):

4. *Visual products exist within a larger body of cultural products which are said to comprise a language* . . . This use of language coincides with movements recognized over time: the language of Minimalism, the language of Expressionism, the language of Modernism.

5. *Means of making objects or images impose restrictions and furnish possibilities* – the language of photography, the language of painting. This can be broader than just medium, as in the language of advertising.

6. *Visual communication is 'universal', pure and unpolluted by words or culture.* One of the most contested beliefs about 'visual language' functions by virtue of assumptions not about language, but about the visual. The assumption is that visual communication speaks across cultures and contexts because it is based on bodily facts shared by everyone – the structure of the eye and brain, the facts of gravity, how we move through space.

7. *The experience of making as an experience of 'speaking through'* . . . This is the sense in which artists, composers, writers and other 'makers' often use it. This version makes an analogy between the act of speaking and the act of making, in that ideas form themselves in the medium's terms. When the medium is thoroughly familiar, like one's native tongue, it may feel transparent as if no act of

'translation' is taking place. Ideas, emotions, inner events form themselves as words, as musical notes, as colours or characters . . . But when one is developing skills and exploring a medium, as when one learns a foreign language, there is often a point at which this 'speaking through' is first experienced. This can be accompanied by feelings of exhilaration, that the dimensions of the medium one is using have themselves become instruments of meaning. 'The music writes itself. There is no longer a composer who pushes the material about, but only its servant, carrying out what the notes themselves imply' (Alexander Goehr quoted in Storr, 1993, p. 96).

Such categorization of different uses of the notion of visual language and visual literacy is important so that various theories and perspectives on the relationship between the visual and the verbal can be placed and understood. Of particular interest to this book are not so much the first three senses outlined above (the visual *as* language) as the last four, which map out a semiotics of the visual in its own terms (as far as is possible) and thus make it comparable with verbal language: the visual *in relation to* verbal language.

From a visual arts point of view, *literacy* is an interesting term to choose to define education in things seen. Allen (1994) charts the recent emergence of the term, 'coming into common use in art education in the 1990s, principally as a result of its appearance in the various documents which led to the publication of the Order for art' (p. 133) and growing from a critical studies movement in the 1980s. He then quotes a definition of visual literacy from Eisner (1989):

By literacy I mean the ability to represent or recover meaning in the variety of forms through which it is made public. In our culture, words, numbers, movements, images, and patterns of sound are forms through which meaning is represented. To read these forms requires an understanding of their rules, their contexts and their syntactical structures. (p. 8)

In other words, this is literacy as metaphor: the suggestion behind the term 'visual literacy' is not literal – that would almost be a contradiction in terms – but metaphorical. That is to say, a broad understanding of 'literacy' as reading and writing, as constituting a semiotic *system*, is used to describe what *could be* a way of accounting for a 'visual grammar'.[1] The source of the metaphor is not only Hoggart in *The Uses of Literacy* (1957), the widely acknowledged stimulus for seeing language in its social and cultural context, but also the very different tradition captured by Chomsky in *Syntactic Structures* (1964). Once Chomsky had attempted – but failed – to identify universal structures in language that were not only applicable to language and the other semiological systems, but to the innate structure of the mind itself, the enterprise of accounting for symbolic systems developed into semiotics: the study of sign systems. The history of the term 'literacy' goes back further, at least to the late nineteenth century, when it was claimed in 1883 that Massachusetts was the first state in the Union in literacy achievement in its native population. The definition given in the *Oxford English Dictionary* is based on a 'knowledge of letters' and on the broadly accepted conception of an ability to read and write.

The definitional emphasis on *rules* and *syntactical structures* in Eisner, as well as on the *contexts* of art forms, suggests that art educators think that there is a firm foundation in language and literacy studies that might inform their own practices. Linguists are not so confident about sentence grammar or syntax, however. Structuralists have tried to secure a reasonable account of the internal structures of language and have given up in the face of the enormous contextual and contingent factors bearing upon language; similarly any attempts to 'teach the grammar' of English in schools as a way to becoming a practitioner in the use of language have failed in the long term because: (a) the grammar is too complex for any other than Linguistics graduates to understand; (b) it just does not work because it is not necessary to learn 'grammar' to become competent and skilful in your native language; and (c) the 'grammar' cited is a grammar of sentence construction. It does not account for the other levels of language like the text level. *Rules* are hopelessly limited (and much of language is not rule governed, though it might be norm oriented), *syntaxes*[2] hard to define and *structures* as much in the eye of the beholder as inherent in the language.

So, when Allen (1994) acknowledges that 'research in the field [of literacy] is problematising the term even as we art teachers appropriate it' (p. 141), his acknowledgement needs to be amplified. No doubt the visual arts world is riven by the same debates as is the world of verbal language. It is dangerous to build on a foundation that is itself shaky, even though one way to look critically at the practices and assumptions in one's own discipline is to compare them with a *seemingly* unified picture in another discipline.

The central unifying concept in helping us to understand the relationship – sometimes of tension, sometimes complementary, always contiguous – between the verbal and visual is the concept of *framing*.

Framing

I will consider first how notions of framing can apply to language and the language arts; second, I will widen the frame to look at the relationship between the visual and verbal; and third, I will reflect on implications for classroom practice in the subject of English.

All language – including poetic language – is transactional, and the framing that goes on both separates and distinguishes different kinds of language from the everyday discourse of the world, and also places it in relation to the everyday world of discourse. The frames both enclose and, because they are metaphorical and not made of wood, *disclose*.

Framing as a metaphor for education in the language arts offers the following: (a) the 'empty space', the arena in which words operate, very like a frame; and (b) the reinforced notion that words are transactional: they are shaped in particular ways in order to *do particular things*.

Just as the levels at which language operates were set out earlier in the book, so too the levels at which language has been analysed have moved through the last six decades from small units to larger ones. In the 1950s, linguists were refining theories about phonology, the sound components in words. They then moved on to morphology, the science of how bits of words – like prefixes, roots and suffixes, i.e. grammatically meaningful micro-units of language, fit together. The logical next step was to study whole words – lexicography – and then came Chomsky, suggesting that syntax, or the ways words were put together in strings, was the key, not only to understanding language, but also to understanding the way the human mind works. After syntax, the focus shifted to the whole sentence, then to strings of sentences, paragraphs, stanzas and so on, and notions of cohesion and coherence in text; thence to study of the 'whole text' and, consequently, a fascination with different types of text, or 'genres'. In the 1990s, we began to see that texts are flexible, varied, more and more mixed media in their composition and dependent upon their context for full comprehension. The interface between the text and its context is the area that linguists and educationalists are concerned with now, hence the need for a closer look at framing. Framing both defines the text – think of the white space around a poem – and gives it 'position' in relation to other texts and less formal language. Framing, crucially, is responsive to context; whereas genre theory, at least in some extreme versions, is not.

The concept of framing as applied to language in interaction is not new. Its first use of this kind in recent times is in Bateson's 'A Theory of Play and Fantasy' in *Ecology of mind* (1954), where it is suggested that 'no communicative move, whether verbal or non-verbal [can] be understood' without reference to the frame of interpretation being applied to it (See also Tannen, 1979). As Tannen suggests, notions of framing have been taken up by researchers in communication, psychology, anthropology and sociology (especially in Goffman's *Frame Analysis*, 1974).

In *Framing and Interpretation*, a recent book from Australia which moves forward the so-called genre debate (linguists vs. educationalists), Gale McLachlan and Ian Reid (1994) quote Frow (1986), who suggests that a frame 'can be anything that acts as a sign of qualitative difference, a sign of the boundary between a marked and an unmarked place' (p. 13). They go on to say that in the case of literary texts, fictional space is thus set off from reality by the use of various framing devices like titles, subtitles and prefaces and specific locations in bookshops and libraries.

The act of framing – the term McLachlan and Reid prefer to use to 'frame' because of its very inscription of action and flexibility – seems a more useful one than 'genre' (when used to mean 'text-type'), in that it describes *acts* rather than *phenomena*; it is flexible, as frames can be adapted and changed according to the needs of the participants within the frame. Metaphors of framing can indicate that 'in order to perceive and understand anything we must provisionally distinguish it from other things while also relating it to them' (1994: 16). It is 'the process of demarcating phenomena in a double-edged way that is simultaneously inclusive and exclusive' (ibid.).

As far as poetry goes, it is now well accepted that the same words that constitute a non-fictional text like a newspaper article, for instance, can also constitute, with some reframing, a poem. Smith (1968) refers to a number of different ways in which a poem might end (her book is called *Poetic Closure*) – repetition of a refrain, by picking up a rhyme from earlier in the poem, with a concluding statement – but, as McLachlan and Reid say, there is no considered theory of framing to emerge from her work: all the focus is on the internal dynamics of the poem.

What is particularly significant here is that formalist notions of literary identity (i.e. an equation for poetry, one for the short story, one for the novel, etc.) 'ignore the paradoxical status of the frame itself . . . and refuse to make the frame work except as a barrier between literature and its contexts' (Carroll, 1987: 145). That is to say, formalist approaches do not recognize the two-way traffic that a frame sets up, and the invigorating nature of that two-way traffic. Frames as barriers set up hierarchical relationships between literature and other kinds of language, between poetry and non-poetic language (whatever that is) and between fiction and non-fiction.

In summary:

- language use is framed, both in speech and writing, both internally and externally;
- the framing is dynamic, bridgeable, capable of being generative; that is why it is currently a more satisfying theory of the production and reception of texts than genre theory;
- those interested in holding on to power and who have a vested interest in hierarchy, however, like to think frames are static;
- some teachers, some curriculum planners teach these forms as if they are static (and their pedagogies are primitive);
- framing is useful in that it makes us think about the borders between fiction and 'non-fiction';
- framing also is a powerful analytical and creative act in a rhetorical view of communication.

Thus a text or image can never escape the multiple frames in which it sits.

What has all this consideration of framing of texts and of the contiguity of word and image got to do with education, and more specifically with classrooms? Think about the institutional and political setting of the classroom. Children go to school – that is enshrined in law – and they spend most of their day sitting in classrooms. These rooms are framed by the school and its locality and ethos, its *mores*. There are rituals attached to the space of the classroom: children might stand behind their desks until a sign from the teacher indicates that they should sit down and the lesson *per se* is to begin. In other classes, the teacher's attempts to start might be hampered. However informal that classroom is, the space defined is one in which *framing is more heightened than outside the classroom*. There may be a globe in the corner; texts may be read – usually not for their intrinsic worth, if there is such a thing, but as learning texts. This is why fiction has had pride of place in the English classroom: not only because it has been central to an education in the humanities since 1921, when Sampson published *English for the English* and saw the subject replacing Classics as the central civilizing force in the curriculum; but also because, in its exploration and depiction of possible worlds, *fiction is like classrooms* in that framing is foregrounded. Fiction is a highly symbolic form, just as classrooms contain symbols of the world outside. Classrooms are thus highly framed spaces, defined not only by their walls (which are significant enough) but also by the tacit frames of language, power and ritual that suggest something different is going on there. Children who rebel against these frames, who try to break the frame – by literally throwing things out of the window, or turning up late, or not turning up at all, or subverting the expected hierarchical order of the room – find learning in these spaces unsatisfactory. They do not wish to play that particular game. At the same time, the really exciting action in classrooms is when the frames are open to the urgency, rhythms and demotic of the language of the world.

Writing and communication that moves beyond the essentially fictional (which is, after all, bound by the book or film) is a threat to the classroom, and to the institutional nature of schooling, because it breaks down the walls of the classroom. It cannot be contained. And yet, at the same time, the skilful English teacher spends much of his/her time moving backwards and forwards between the worlds of fiction and the 'real worlds' in which the student operates.

In further summary, then:

- framing is helpful to the language arts, coming as it does from sociological theory, because: (a) it takes us beyond the sterile debate on genre; (b) it is flexible, dynamic, rhetorical and keyed in to people; and (c) because it links English again with the other arts – dance, theatre, music, art, design, architecture, etc.;
- what goes on inside frames is in urgent need of study and research, particularly the contiguity of the verbal and visual;
- but what frames do when they come up against each other is also interesting. This phenomenon suggests a non-narrative kind of communication, linking composition to reading/reception in a more collage-like way than we have been used to;

- framing also helps us to see what we do now, and the shortcomings of it. The overemphasis on teaching fiction in English classrooms, or, to put it another way, the misunderstanding of the relationship between fiction and documentary, has blinkered us as English teachers to the possibilities and importance of argument/dialogue, and the importance of going beyond the classroom if we are to educate children fully in language;
- framing is an important element in a rhetorical theory of communication, privileging neither the visual nor verbal, but accepting that they complement each other in the making of meaning.

The nature of 'visual literacy': problems and possibilities for the classroom

To anticipate the next chapter, one of the main frames within which the convergence takes place is provided by computer screens and/or television screens (which themselves are becoming increasingly interdependent). Just as wordprocessing, searching databases and computer literacy are becoming more commonplace in English, so too art educators are looking at monitors as well as at paintings. As Allen (1994) notes (p. 134): 'However much we might like to claim a more significant place for practices like painting and drawing or ceramics and printmaking, we cannot pretend that they are as common in people's daily lives as the visual artefacts of the mass media', like cinema and broadcast television. Critical awareness in the face of screens seems to be one of the goals of the educators in visual literacy. Another is a heightened awareness of the links between being critical and being creative. Like *critical literacy*, the emphasis on not being duped by the media is a strong one,[3] and the recognition is that drawing, painting and allied arts and crafts are not sufficient in themselves to educate children and young people for the world out there. Of course, computer screens are not the only place where there is a dynamic relationship between word and image: magazines, newspapers, children's books all combine the two semiotic systems.

A map of verbal and visual kinds of communication

Which media do we use to communicate? The following table suggests that perhaps the norm is a combination of the verbal and the visual (i.e. the second and third columns):

Visual	Visual/written	Visual/spoken	Written	Spoken
Art galleries[4] 'Pure' landscape[5]	Comics	Most television	Most novels	Telephone conversations
	Most recipe books	Most film	Most academic articles	
	Catalogues	Face-to-face conversation	Most email	
	Magazines			
	Newspapers			
	Multimedia programs			
	Children's books			
	Non-fiction works			
	Manuals			
	Most advertisements			

It should be clear from even a crude listing of this kind[6] that most communication takes place simultaneously in more than one medium, and that certainly the popular forms of communication combine the visual with the verbal. Books and journals on the subject of the relationship of word to image – like *Word & Image*[7] – are always well received in literary and artistic circles, but do not give a real indication of the vast interrelationship between word and image that most of us take for granted.

Visual *rhetoric*?

A better approach to visual literacy or the frame in which the visual and the verbal are converging, and in which the contiguities between them create a new dynamic, is via a contemporary conception of 'rhetoric'. 'Contemporary' distinguishes rhetoric from its Aristotelian version and defines its area of interest as informed by cultural studies, linguistics and theories of dialogue. It is political, tying personal expressiveness to notions of audience and the media of communication; it is also a down-to-earth, pragmatic way of thinking about how best to frame a message in a real situation. Rather than repeat arguments I have set out elsewhere (Andrews, 1992b, 1995), here is a summary of the advantages of seeing the verbal (both spoken and written) and visual – and the tactile and dramatic/gestural – as coming under the umbrella of rhetoric:

- Rhetoric is socially and politically situated. It sees communication as taking place between a creator/ speaker/ 'rhetor' and his/her/their audience in a particular situation. The situation partly determines the 'meaning', as do the creator and the audience. It is thus not prey to theories of 'reader response' or 'author-centred ideology' or Marxist social analysis because it embraces all three perspectives.
- A rhetorical perspective allows the production and analysis of different media alongside each other, as the level it operates at is one of communication, action and purpose. It brings reading and composition closer together in the way that speaking and listening were in classical rhetoric (the 'art of persuasion'). If art educators are concerned about a separation between the tactile/expressive domain on the one hand, and the critical domain on the other, a rhetorical perspective unites the two – and does so in a way which, although powerful theoretically, is also very pragmatic and practical.
- Crucially, for those of us concerned with education, rhetoric mirrors the natural learning situation in which education is an effect of community – the most common one in which children learn to read (in the fullest sense of that word): a situation in which the visual and verbal are rarely far apart.
- By perceiving schools and art galleries as rhetorical communities, we are freed to see them in a wider context of social communities in general: families, local community groups, nations, international communities, electronic communities, communities whose sensibilities are determined by television or radio. Such liberation from the confines of the classroom or gallery/museum widens the possibilities for learning, and also allows us to see the value of classrooms and galleries, framed as they are with particular functions and by particular ideologies.[8]

- Rhetoric foregrounds argument, allowing positioning in relation to existing works and questioning of them to take place more readily than in conventional approaches.
- A rhetorical perspective provides a theoretical unity to the verbal and visual arts (arts of communication, arts of discourse) at a time when they need to defend and justify their presence in the curriculum.
- Rhetoric does not privilege one art form over another, nor one medium of expression over another. It both allows image and text to stand alongside each other and their relationship to be analysed; and it throws new light on, for instance, the relationship between fiction and documentary.[9]
- More practically, rhetoric might help in providing a language to describe the elements, relations and functions of a multimedia screen.

Two articles from *Rebirth of Rhetoric* (Andrews, 1992b): Patsy Stoneman's 'Reading Across Media: The Case of *Wuthering Heights*' and Prudence Black and Stephen Muecke's 'The Power of a Dress: The Rhetoric of a Moment in Fashion', drive home the importance of an umbrella-like perspective on visual and verbal communication. Stoneman traces the development of visual images derived from the novel, suggesting that the novel is transformed completely in the process. Black and Muecke analyse a photograph of Jean Shrimpton at the 1965 Melbourne Cup, using the notion from Barthes of the rhetoric of the image.

Given the exciting potential of analysis and production of word and image, perhaps a rhetorical perspective is the best one to take if we are not only to understand what is happening to us as we read from computer screens, but also to compose more effectively and to develop our own (and our students' and children's) use and awareness of the range of discourse communities in which verbal and visual languages are learnt.

Questions for further research

I take it as given that most printed and electronic communication (at least in popular culture) is now verbal/visual, rather than purely verbal or purely visual. Indeed, purely verbal communication (*London Review of Books, Oxford English Dictionary*, etc.) is rare, and if we go further along the spectrum of the verbal/visual to the very end, we would be hard pressed to find verbal communication that is not associated with the visual in some way. Radio is perhaps a classic exception (though radio is an interesting case in that we always seem to be doing something else while listening to it; the senses, the body is engaged in some other tangentially related way). Printed verbal communication almost always has a visual dimension of some sort that helps the reader frame it. Similarly, at the other end of the spectrum, where do we find unmediated, 'pure' visual communication? Certainly not in cities, which are verbal language-rich, but perhaps in uninscribed landscape, in images that are language-free and also unmediated by language.

Perhaps, if you follow the argument of Richard Lanham and his notion of 2,000 years of multimedia, it has always been the case that the verbal and visual work together. To quote Lanham, 'pure' printed written communication (to be more precise) operates via an 'aesthetic of denial'; as if, outside the frame of the black-and-white printed page, colour, texture and tone are desperate to get in.

But where, in this welter of the verbal/visual, are the really interesting areas for research? What is the exact nature of that relationship in these interesting areas? What is the evidence of how children bring together the verbal and visual, and what are the implications for language learning? And, finally, what model of communication might best account for and generate new insights into the relationship between the verbal and visual in communication?

What model of communication best suits a world in which email, multimedia, old-fashioned print, speech, and so on are prevalent; in which the *managing* of communication for people at work is close to defining what work actually is; in which children and adults, education and the workplace are making sense of digital data in verbal and visual form, often simultaneously in the same message? That discipline in which such a model finds its home might be linguistics, but a linguistics much transformed. Single-channel linguistics (i.e. linguistics based only on a study of verbal language in speech or writing) must surely wither into obscurity as it increasingly ceases to represent the real contexts of language use. Multi-channel linguistics – almost a contradiction in terms – is a different animal. It won't be concerned so much with the internal dynamics of one channel or mode, but with the relationship between different channels or modes and their relationship with their functional contexts. In the history of linguistics over the last fifty years, that seems a logical enough step, but we have now come to a point – helped by linguistics' charting of the levels of language description and their relationships to each other – where we have to step beyond linguistics.

The bridge to a new model is offered in Deborah Tannen's *Framing in Discourse* (1993), though the analysis in the essays belongs to the old paradigm that is sociolinguistics based. In this collection there are a number of essays – mostly by graduate students at Georgetown University – which give excellent analyses of discourse. Their strength but also their limitation is that they are single channelled. What does emerge, at a more general level, is the idea that frames (brought into discourse analysis from sociology, and borrowed metaphorically from the art world) can be useful ways of making sense and also of creating communication, however many channels are used.

In opera for example, the heavy framing (opera as social institution, high cost of tickets, ornate theatres, lavish costumes and sets, the often huge frames of the singers, the bringing together of song, recitative, music and acting) allows for a multi-channelled, highly formal art work. In conversation across a kitchen table between two adults, framed by social conventions of marriage and/or partnership and/or friendship, a cup of tea, the table, the room, the house, communication is going to be of a different order. Different kinds of dialogue exist in the two situations; different channels are used (if there is a printed or hand-written letter between the two conversants, the social and communi-cative dynamic is changed yet again). In each case, the framing partly determines the nature of communication. At the same time, the frame can always be broken, transgressed for comical or revolutionary effect, or simply to enhance the awareness of the frame. In my own tentative, emergent model of literacy learning, while I would put considerable emphasis on framing both in the teaching of reading and writing, I would not hesitate to go along with children of any age who want to subvert, transgress, change the frame in order to inject some humour, energy and fun into the process.

Frames are not the same as genres; that is why I prefer the term 'framing' to 'frames'. Framing is an act, not a tangible thing. It is called into play in order to give historical credence and shape to an encounter, that is to give it 'meaning'. Even genres conceived as social action rather than text-type do not convey for me the fluidity and flexibility of framing. But framing of itself is not sufficient for a model, because frames come in different shapes and sizes and natures according to their contexts. Framing is, however, the agent of action and cohesion (and coherence) in a theory of communication underpinned by rhetoric.

The shift away from semiotics and language-based theories of communication towards rhetorical theories has been marked recently. Contingency, the move away from modernist systematizing of communication and a need for a more grounded model of communication have contributed to this shift. It marks not so much a turn to the visual as a return to a *modus operandi* in which channels of communication – the visual, the aural, the physical – and modes of communication – speech, writing, other visual modes, dance – are considered alongside each other: an acceptance of the multimedia nature of most communication, whether electronically driven or not. Mitchell indicates this shift in the prefatory notes to 'What is Visual Culture?' (1986: 208), where he records how a faculty working group on visual culture at the University of Chicago in 1993 rejected an emphasis on semiotics and sign theory as a starting point 'in favor of an introduction that would stress visual experience as its point of departure'. The first point to emerge from such a paradigm shift is that it is partly brought about by the breaking down of the separation of humanistic disciplines into 'verbal' and 'visual' camps along with the distinction between high art and mass culture; this breaking down of walls has implications for both the verbal and visual.

In relation to framing in the macro-sense of institutional programming and the design of courses for schools and universities, Mitchell's observation that it is the permeable boundaries between the various 'insides' or 'outsides' of disciplines that are most noticeable in the study of culture in the late twentieth century is a salient one:

> One can deplore these developments as a degradation of eternal standards, or as the predictable corruption of advanced capitalism; one can celebrate them as the hyper-fun of advanced postmodernism. Or one can do neither, and attempt to assess dialectically and historically the contemporary relations of artistic institutions to what lies outside them in what I have been calling 'visual culture'. This will not rescue us from the contradictions of what Panofsky calls an 'organic situation', but it might provide a way of making those contradictions the very subject matter of the field, rather than embarrassments to be finessed in the name of disciplinary coherence. (1986: 217)

The case of photography

A number of action research projects in the 1990s, again funded by the Arts Council, indicate the power of photography in developing the English curriculum. Three of these are recorded in Walton (1995), Brake (1996) and Sinker (1997). The first of these, culminating in *Picture My World*, provides ample evidence for the power and use of photographs in the primary English curriculum. The mini-action research projects which are reported took place in schools around England, using photography in different ways to engage children in the art of photography and in the service of English and other subjects. The book also provides many examples of practical activities that can be tried in the classroom. Similarly, Brake's book *Changing Images* records and discusses project work in four secondary schools in the Manchester area. What is striking about both books (and the projects they report) is the innovations that took place in the schools, resulting from collaborations between artists/photographers, teachers and pupils. In particular, the use of digital imaging and the manipulation of such images separately from, or alongside, conventionally produced images point towards new practice in the classroom.

The Rosendale Odyssey project took this way of working yet further. It started as a project in which a primary school in Brixton, south London, wanted to celebrate its centenary. The initial conception was to ask young children (6–7-year-olds) to find out about their own families' histories. Many of these involved contacting grandparents in other countries, and all involved collecting photographs from family albums, letters and other memorabilia. These were used as the basis for website design and creation, assisted by artists and researchers as well as the school's teachers. The result is a stunning cornucopia of images, stories and mixed media works with which the children communicated with children in other countries via email.

Another research project which Sinker evaluated in the 1990s was the Media Education through Art Progression Project at George Orwell School in Islington, north London (Sinker, 1998). This project, conceived by Kathy Stonier and Kate Kelley and involving a number of photographers and artists in digital media, consisted of a range of activities for students in the 11–14 age group. Under a broad theme of personal and cultural identities, students from a variety of cultural backgrounds experimented with work at the borders of art and design, media studies and literacy. The aim of the evaluation was 'partly to determine the success of the project (its processes and approaches) and partly to track the progression of the students themselves through their development and participation' (p. 2). Two of the teachers involved in the project commented:

> [The students] see lots of different contemporary stuff on the television and in films, and I think that really informs the way they think of and see things – especially all the experimental stuff that's come out of pop video in the last ten years . . . framing images, thinking about how images go together, organizing images and changing them, cutting and pasting them on screen . . . Their visual literacy skills have developed a lot.
>
> Visual literacy has been developed through the range of skills that they feel comfortable with or would want to use. And also through ideas and finding different ways of being able to express those ideas. I think it makes them question conventions more. For instance now if they look at the work of a specific artist they might question 'Why did he do it this way? Why did he use this technique? How else could he have done it?' That questioning has come about because of their knowledge and experience of different media. (Sinker, 1998: 15)

The project as a whole gave the students involved more confidence in themselves, and in terms of themselves as artists; teachers developed their professional skills; and students' sense of audience was enhanced. Sinker quotes (p. 19) the British Film Institute's curriculum statement for secondary media education: 'media education enhances art education in its understanding of how a text's form defines its likely conventions. It also informs art about patronage and social productions of art, describing practice as less the preserve of "geniuses" or in a limited range of forms e.g. drawing or painting, but more about each child's ability to make meaning in a wide variety of cultural forms and media products.' This statement on media education leads us on to consider the role of the moving image in English education.

The moving image

Film and video have been the Cinderellas of school subject English for over a generation, despite the efforts of the British Film Institute and other similar bodies. The reasons for this exclusion of the moving image from mainstream English are several: the lack of facilities to show films – especially short films – in schools; a less than coherent account of how development in moving image education takes place; and an ignorance among English teachers about the nature and application of the moving image. The principal reason, however, is probably that the majority of English teachers still see themselves as working within a personal growth/literary paradigm.

Resistance is likely to change in the light of the report *Making Movies Matter* (Bazalgette *et al.*, 1999). This extensive report, which is the work of the Film Education Working Group, 'calls for a new attitude towards the moving image amongst education policy-makers' who 'should recognize that critical and creative moving image skills will be a key element of literacy in the 21st century' (p. 2). The arguments for an increased and central recognition of moving image in the curriculum are based not only on conviction and the sense that the time has come for film and video to take a more central cultural role in education, but also on research. Some of the main findings are summarized below:

- Research on young people's uses of video 'found that although teenagers are more likely to watch films on television than in the cinema, over 60% said they preferred to watch them at the cinema' (p. 10).
- In France, film education is more developed than in the UK. The Enfants de Cinema scheme, for instance, 'provided cinema visits for nearly 610,000 schoolchildren and 15,000 teachers in more than half the country's departments' in 1997/8. It operates at three levels: the Ecoles et Cinema for primary schools, the Collège au Cinema for lower secondary, and the Lycéens au Cinema for upper secondary.
- Europa Cinemas, a scheme run from Paris, supports 'some 800 screens in 200 locations throughout Europe' with funding partly conditional on evidence of 'activities directed towards young people' (p. 24).
- In terms of 'cineliteracy', the four competences necessary for moving image education are analytical competence, contextual knowledge, canonical knowledge and production competence (p. 31).

- The BFI's 1998 *Audit of Media in English* 'revealed that, although 91% of the sample of 718 secondary English teachers in England and Wales were enthusiastic about media teaching and 43% claimed to devote between 10% and 25% of curriculum time to it, most of this work was likely to relate to print texts. 44% wanted the curricular requirement clarified and 75% wanted more training in how to teach it. Teachers feel most confident about teaching film versions of novels and plays, and less so with teaching about film in its own right' (p. 33).

- The *Audit* also noted that 'of the 718 English teachers surveyed . . . all of whom carry a statutory requirement to pay some sort of attention to "media" in their teaching, only 7% had a media-related qualification in their first degree and only 10% had had media-related elements in their initial teacher training' (p. 50).

- A commissioned review of a range of teaching resources for 5–18-year-olds found that 'the uncertain status of moving image education' in the curriculum has had damaging effects on the promotion of such education. First, in that publishers are not willing to commit resources to projects which they see as of minority interest; and second, in that 'film education resources are addressed to undertrained and unconfident teachers and thus need to teach them directly as well as providing them with materials for students' (p. 68). Shortcomings of existing resources include their presentation, which often considered the content more than the audience; inaccessibility and lack of passion; lack of clarity of learning outcomes; and a preponderance of resources that attempt to teach *about* film rather than *through* film.

Research undertaken for the Film Education Working Group found that people working in the moving image sector feel isolated and value the opportunity to share practice and learn about the practice of others. They would welcome a more coherent national and regional strategy to bring together access, research, training and implementation issues so that their experience could be enhanced and also better used to help young people learn more about the moving image.

One specific example of research into the use of moving image is that by Sefton-Green and Parker (2000). In particular, the research was intended to form the basis for further studies into the ways 'in which children might benefit from having opportunities to edit moving images' (p. 5). Since the early 1980s, editing has been an important element in the skills necessary for the drafting of written compositions, but like other aspects of media education, editing moving images has not played such a central role. Sefton-Green and Parker describe the process of 'technical processes, from changing text in a word-processing package to cutting up strips of film or, most relevant for research, using digital programs in non-linear editing. At the same time, it also refers to an intellectual process: how we summarise or cut down larger units of text or story' (p. 64). Good examples of software teaching and learning materials on editing include Simons *et al.* (1996) and BFI (1997), both of which use varying degrees of arrangement and editing of images and film and are aimed at the 11–18-year-old age range. The research found no specific software for the younger age range on editing images, but a range of programs of various kinds, like *KidPix Studio, Magic Artist* and *The Complete Animator,* which were trialled with Year 1 and Year 5 classes. The authors argue that editing took place in both deep and superficial ways, both in the arrangement and rearrangement of images that make up an animation or film, and also in the surface management of presentation. At the deeper level, arrangement and editing constitute a manifestation of cognition.

Implications for practice

The 'turn to the visual', however seriously we take this phrase to indicate a sea-change in communicative practice in contemporary societies across the world, has implications for the practice of teaching English. First, there is a need to recognize that popular genres such as comics, magazines and newspapers have been combining the verbal and visual for decades. Second, that the contiguity of image and text is a fundamental design feature of such communication and that this very contiguity is a subject for reflection and making in the classroom. All too often, in English classrooms, the visual is secondary to the creation of text (and therefore as a result sometimes of very low quality). We need to move to a position where the visual takes equal status alongside the verbal in communicative compositions.

The implications of such a move are considerable, not only for the initial and continuing development of teachers, but for policy formation and especially for bodies which are entrusted with the assessment of progress in language. In more detail, some of these implications are:

- 'English' as a subject will have to rethink itself to embrace the visual and other modes of communication;
- still and moving image education will become part of the education in initial and continuing development for teachers;
- theoretical models for describing and explaining the nature of English as a subject will need to be redrawn;
- classrooms for design and communication will need to be re-thought. The most obvious solution is a classroom of state-of-the-art multimedia computers, with spaces in the room or the school for composition of a more conventional kind (e.g. large tables for design, manual cutting-and-pasting) and spaces for discussion, group work, etc. Facilities for showing film and video will have to be considered, so that they can be woven more easily into the fabric of lessons.

Notes

1   Literacy is currently being used in a number of fields to describe both the semiotic systems used in those fields and the language used to talk about them. See, for example, Barnett (1994) on technological literacy. There is, of course, nothing wrong with using the term literacy in a metaphorical way.

2   Syntaxes do not work outside language and computer programs because they imply fixed units (words) with relatively tightly defined meanings. One of the shortcomings of Chomskian syntactic linguistics was that it tried to account for language through syntactic structures, when meaning in fact derives from the whole composition within a social context. There is a danger that a visual literacy based on a syntax of art will look only within the frame, not at the nature of the frame and what that suggests about the relationship of signs within the frame to those without it. Eisner does not appear to understand this aspect of language.

3   There still seems to be a prevalent Leavisite attitude towards the media that we need to *protect* ourselves against it rather than enjoy and appreciate it, as we do literature.

4   Most galleries are full of words as well as images. Galleries like Kettle's Yard in Cambridge and the Frick Collection in New York are exceptions in that they resist the temptation to mediate art works through language.

5   Artists like Ian Hamilton Finlay deliberately place 'words' and other linguistic icons in landscape to debunk the conception of a pure uninscribed landscape.

6   Like all category lists, this is an over-simplification. Conventions can be subverted, and there is plenty of overlap or combination possible between these categories. The *function* of this map, however, is to reinforce the predominant presence of the visual/written in printed communication.

7   *Word & Image*, a quarterly journal of verbal/visual enquiry, published by Taylor & Francis, 11 New Fetter Lane, London EC4P 4EE.
8   See Bazerman (1994).
9   Rhetoric can cope with a challenging art installation like Camerawork's 'A-baa', in which, on 18 November 1995, a live audio transmission of a sheep grazing in a field in Devon was relayed to a 'white gallery' in London 'for the listener to ruminate over'. The audience was also invited to graze on written thoughts related to the installation on the World Wide Web.

Chapter 7

ICT in English and Literacy

There is relatively little research on the impact of information and communication technologies on learning and teaching in English. This is probably because ICT has moved fast, especially since 1990 and the more widespread use of the Internet. Research, by comparison, has a slower gestation: there have to be extensive reviews of the literature, careful pilot studies to test methodology, intensive and/or comprehensive surveys and considered writing-up. It is hard to complete a thorough research study with significant results in a year (only those on Masters programmes and TTA teacher research grants can begin to attempt that, and their results are almost always tentative and in need of further research); a more reasonable timescale is two to three years, with three to five years for larger projects. And in three to five years not only might ICT advance rapidly and far, but the infrastructure and use of it might also change radically.

It has thus been practice for government departments and others interested in gauging the impact of ICT on learning to commission short-term evaluations of new developments, rather than invest in medium- to long-term research. Evaluations in themselves are useful: they employ research methods, but they do have to be read critically to ensure that they have been carried out disinterestedly.

However, there has been some important work done. Publications of particular interest to language and English teachers include Snyder (1996), Harrison *et al.* (1998), Moseley and Higgins (1999) and Goodwyn (2000a). In a special issue of *English in Education* in 1997 (Andrews, 1997b), Tweddle takes a retrospective look at developments in ICT in English in the years 1981 to 1996. This is an important article, as it summarizes not only the government initiatives in a period which saw England and Wales moving towards the highest ratio of computers to students in primary and secondary classrooms worldwide, but also the short-term thinking that accompanied such an enthusiastic deployment of hardware. Early (i.e. the first half of the 1980s) use of computers in English classrooms was as wordprocessors. English teachers saw that the computer enabled drafts of writing to be made and remade with relative ease, removing the tedious writing-out that was necessitated by successive drafts in handwriting. Thus two developments in English teaching fed each other in this period, both at primary and secondary level: on the one hand, the emerging understanding that the processes of writing could be understood and taught via deep as well as superficial drafting; and on the other, the advent of a tool that enabled drafts to be made with ease. Tweddle notes:

> As teachers reflected on the way computers were used in their classrooms they repeatedly made the same observations. The early anecdotal evidence suggested that computers could support collaboration, creativity, independent learning, reflection, real and authentic purposes, pupils acting as experts, talk for learning. (1997: 6)

That last potential benefit – computers as aids to talking for learning – came about by the fact that often students in secondary classrooms had to share a computer with one or two other students. When they were composing in small groups, the ostensible reason for the activity was to work on drafts of material and compose collaboratively. The most telling benefit, however, turned out to be the talk that accompanied com-position: talk that was sharply focused on the details of composition, from the arrangement of the text, the style and register in which it was written and its content, to surface features such as spelling and punctuation.

After an initial flush of enthusiasm from English teachers, they soon came to see that ICT was only used within English when it could make a distinctive and important contribution to realizing the objectives of the English curriculum. Key areas in which it was effective were seen to be in drafting and reaching authentic audiences (through the presentation of printed letters and other documents); cloze exercises (especially the justly famous 'Developing Tray' software developed by Bob Moy at The

English Centre in London) where text emerged gradually with student input, as if from a photographer's developing tray; and in promoting collaborative and well-focused talk. Tweddle draws out the implications of 'Developing Tray' for the English curriculum as a whole. As well as being a superb way to reveal the nature of a particular text, she saw in it a model for the teaching of reading more generally, based on prediction and bringing your own experience as a reader to the text.

In the same issue of *English in Education* in which Tweddle's retrospective article takes pole position, there are other articles of interest. Stannard (1997) explores the language, structure and imagery of the Internet, suggesting that as well as being a rich source of information, the Net offers 'new ways of seeing and engaging with the world' (p. 14) and also acts as 'a kind of meta-text itself which has mythopoeic resonances' (ibid.). Leach (1997) gives an account of how trainee English teachers at the Open University used email and a course website to create a community of discourse which enhanced their early forays into teaching the subject and at the same time provided for them a community of learners which gave them a strong sense of being part of a profession. Goodwyn *et al.* (1997) chart the shift in attitude among English teachers to the new technologies, recording that in the late 1990s 'the majority of student teachers and about half of serving teachers of English' (p. 54) welcomed ICT as a central and integral part of the subject, as opposed to a more resistant attitude earlier in the decade.

In this chapter, I will concentrate on the more practically oriented articles in the issue of the journal. Snyder (1997) focuses on hypertext, 'the technology that makes possible nonsequential, fully electronic reading and writing' (p. 23), and in particular hyperfiction. More specifically, hyperfiction is composed not in the sequential form of the codex book – page by page in a particular order – but more like a three-dimensional collage of texts through which the reader can navigate according to his or her own will. Unless they have a map to the text as a whole, the reader will often embark on a hypertextual narrative without knowing how 'long' it is and certainly without an ending in sight. In such a role, the reader plays a more active part in the construction of the narrative than in conventional book-reading; he or she makes the narrative sequence by the associative moves he/she makes. Beginnings and endings – so important to the psychological shape of a conventional narrative, and reinforced by Aristotle's 'the end is everything' – are suspended and then determined by the reader. Throughout the article there is the caveat that a new textual configuration like hypertext will not necessarily supersede the printed book. Rather, it is likely to stand alongside the book as a different form of expression, just as the invention of print did not herald the demise of handwriting; or the wax cylinder (precursor of the record and CD-ROM), just over a hundred years ago, which despite the early hype, did not supplant the book.

Darby *et al.* (1997) 'describe the insights gained by a group of primary teachers investigating the implications of CDRom for English' (p. 34) with 7–11-year-old students. One of these was that it is not realistic to think of asking students to 'think of their questions first' before exploring the CD-ROMs. Rather, bringing a critical awareness, honed by computer games and television, to the exploration of the information and structure of CD-ROMs was a more fruitful approach. One teacher (Reid) found that her students became aware of the limits of CD-ROM technology as they used it, having recourse to the book to find supplementary information they thought they would find on the CD. She also found that the skills needed to use the CD-ROM effectively included opening directories and files; dragging saved work into files; saving pictures, sound and text; altering screen mode; editing text and editing pictures. These compositional and management skills are interesting developments from those thought to be essential at the beginning of the 1980s. Another teacher (Dennison) affirms the value of collaborative group work with spin-offs in the quality of typed presentation, a communal sense of ownership and a sheer enjoyment in engaging with the CD-ROM to research and re-present work on a particular topic.

One of the interesting benefits of the introduction of computers into classrooms has been the creation of new modes of text production. This in itself can give rise to opportunities for learning, if you accept that learning in classrooms is often undertaken by the translation or transformation of one 'text' into another. In its simplest form (and very much a technology and pedagogical approach of the 1950s), hearing words and then writing them down involves such transformation. The 'text' is processed by the brain in the transformation. Most work in English classrooms involves translating from text to text: you read a passage from a novel, say, and then answer questions on it or re-present it as a diary entry in the first person. But what multimedia technology allows students and teachers to do is make the transitions between many more different channels of communication – speech, music, images (still and moving), text – and between different genres and forms, some of which are relatively 'pure' and most of which are hybrid. The fact that transformation of some sort *has* to take place for learning to be registered is important: just copying out or downloading text is not much of a learning experience. Re-creating text, re-purposing it for a different audience, changing the channel of communication, genre and form of the text, combining it with other elements in a new composition: all these are creative and liberating activities which ICT has further encouraged. In a summary of the article on teachers' action research in the use of CD-ROMs in primary classrooms, Darby *et al.* (1997: 44) set out the key advances for the subject:

- In the area of speaking and listening, children are negotiating, justifying choices, making decisions and making oral presentations of their work.
- They are reading text on screen . . . reading images . . . selecting relevant information and reading critically. Children supplemented CDRom with other sources when they needed to.
- They are editing and redrafting; adding to and modifying text; adapting text and graphics for a different audience or a different purpose.

The impact of portables

Although not research on English teaching specifically, an evaluation for the British Educational Communications and Technology Agency (Harrison *et al.*, 1998) has much significance for English teaching. Harrison himself is a specialist in reading, and his background contributed much to the nature of the evaluation. Early in 1996, the DfEE asked BECTa to manage a pilot project which aimed to develop teacher competence in the use of ICT. In the first phase of the project, from January 1996 to July 1997, 1,150 primary and secondary teachers were provided with a multimedia portable computer with core software, a number of CD-ROM titles and Internet connection. The evaluation used three sources of data: the BECTa database on teachers using the equipment, a detailed questionnaire administered twice during the project and case-study material based on interviews with 60 teachers. In general, the key findings were that 98 per cent of teachers made effective use of their computers, that their confidence and competence changed for the better, that their knowledge of ICT had increased substantially and that enthusiasm had also increased. Of all the teachers in the experiment, over 90 per cent found that wordprocessing, use of a printer in association with the computer and use of CD-ROMs were the most successful applications, followed by use of the Internet and of spreadsheets. The more visual/graphic side of computer use, like desktop publishing and paint/draw software, was least used.

The key conditions for success were, according to the evaluation, initial and immediate success with the technology; personal ownership and exclusive use of the hardware over an extended period; portability; and a combination of formal and informal support. Conversely, the factors which impeded successful use were initial and/or sustained hardware problems; low confidence; failure to receive promised release time for in-service development; and difficulties with Internet access.

In English, teachers' prior and professional use 'had been mainly word processing' (ibid., p. 13) but all such teachers taking part in the project 'showed significant gains in confidence and were extremely positive about what they had gained' (p. 14). Use of the Internet by English teachers was extensive, with some teachers finding particularly useful material for teaching advanced students (e.g. in the 16–18 age range). As described above (Darby _et al._, 1997), 'CDRom use was perhaps the most significant area of development for teachers and had the greatest impact on use with pupils' (p. 14). Examples of teachers working with students on desktop publishing or Powerpoint-type applications were less common, as was the use of spreadsheets (found in only one teacher – one who had responsibility for managing assessment across the school for 11–14-year-olds). It may have been this teacher who provided the basis for the detailed case study on an English teacher appended to the report. As reports tend to have a limited shelf-life, I quote extensively from this case study here in order to preserve its lessons for a wider audience. It provides an exemplary case of someone who was not particularly confident in ICT use in English at the beginning of the project, but who made great advances during the project.

Marion 'had an old BBC [computer – developed in the 1980s] at home and was "fairly competent" with this . . . She used it to teach basic IT in her previous school' (Darby _et al._, 1997: 52). She had started a qualification in ICT skills but had 'given up when she got on to spreadsheets'. She hadn't used email or the Web before the pilot project, and mainly used computers for producing worksheets. She had used Developing Tray and, other than that, had mostly used wordprocessing with pupils. What she found during the project was that the key factor for her was having time to explore the potential of the computer and link it to her existing work as an English teacher. Consequently, she found herself working at weekends exploring websites and adapting material for use with students in class. She was moving slowly from using the wordprocessor and computer as a glorified typing machine (and thus translating all information into print for further use in the classroom) to beginning to use the portable computer itself for small group work by students. Clearly, one of the issues to emerge from the project was how best to manage the computer in the classroom; and clearly the dynamic and potential use of the computer changes as the number of machines per student changes.

Language use in primary schools was much more likely to see collaboration between teachers, and use in the classroom by students in pair or small-group work, particularly via CD-ROM. Internet use was less extensive than in secondary schools, but display work using desktop publishing applications was more widely used. One distinctive area of development recorded in the evaluation was the professional development of primary teachers. In the following extract from the report, there is an account of how two teachers used the portable machines for their own development:

> Both teachers have a commitment to collaborative research and seek to use the portable computer to support this. Ingrid uses the Internet virtually every night and at weekends. She has put in a great deal of time (and doesn't begrudge it) and her learning has been fast. Her home phone bill has doubled: 'I'm working with teachers in Kentucky and Louisiana' via AOL. She now has her own home page. Phil is going to join an NFER [National Foundation for Educational Research] on-line conference on school improvement and is also interested in collaborative action enquiry with Internet contacts. He is shortly to visit Ireland with an EU [European Union] funded project and wanted to prepare for the visit. (p. 58)

ICT and literacy in primary schools

Perhaps the most reliable recent research into the effectiveness of ICT in the teaching of literacy was that by researchers at the Universities of Durham and Newcastle (Moseley and Higgins, 1999). The full report reviews and summarizes the findings of a research and development project investigating effective pedagogy, provides information about the main stages of the research process and 'provides illustrations of effective practice rich enough to encompass the complexity of the choices teachers have made in deciding when, when not and how to use ICT to strengthen their teaching in literacy' (p. 4). The research 'was conducted using a range of methods which included identifying a sample of teachers using relative performance or "value-added" data from the Performance Indicators in Primary Schools project (PIPS) and survey data to establish degrees of use of ICT in the classroom' (p. 7). Classroom observations were conducted and teachers interviewed. Once baselines were established, various intervention strategies were used and a range of methods employed to track and evaluate these interventions. Researchers found that existing literature had demonstrated that there were three areas on which to focus: the capacity of computers to present or represent ideas dynamically; the facility for providing feedback to students as they were working; and the capacity to present information in easily changeable forms.

The report gives an account of developmental (or intervention) work with students aged between 7 and 10, including presenting texts and supporting writing; improving reading and spelling with speech feedback; developing story-writing skills; teaching the corrective use of omissive apostrophes; reading challenging texts with speech and dictionary support; and using short rhymes to enhance reading comprehension. There is insufficient space in this book to do justice to the range and detail offered in the full report, but important themes emerge from the research. One of these is that primary schools found the speech to text facility of valuable use with children of all abilities in the classroom, especially for reinforcing connections between letters and sounds. There was much more use of Powerpoint-like presentation by both teachers and students, and much less dependence on the translation of digital information to print. It is as if, in the three years between the Multimedia Portables project described above and the project described here, English teaching had made a shift from print to a digital-based understanding of the formats in which language takes shape – with resultant implications for pedagogy and classroom management. Development work in this project took into account a number of factors, including teachers' subject knowledge, their ICT skills and students' ICT skills. It was found that statistically significant gains were made in all the particular subprojects – not attributable to ICT equipment alone, but to its effective use in the classroom with enthusiastic, knowledgeable teachers. Interestingly – and not surprisingly – teachers who favour ICT

> are likely to have well-developed ICT skills and to see ICT as an important tool for learning and instruction. They are also likely to value collaborative working, enquiry and decision-making by pupils. Teachers who have reservations about using ICT are likely to exercise a high degree of direction and to prefer pupils to work individually. (Moseley and Higgins, 1999: 97).

This finding suggests that willingness to use ICT in the service of English, and effectiveness in the use of it, is as much to do with the value-system and ideology of the teacher as with surface characteristics like ICT competence. Your view of English as a subject is more likely to affect your attitude toward the application of ICT in language education than exposure to ICT is to affect your viewpoint. It follows that training and professional development for primary teachers in the application of ICT to literacy teaching must address the values and ideologies underpinning practice as well as technical and pedagogic skills.

Other recent research into primary and pre-school education includes Andrews (1998a), a case study of a 4-year-old's graphic and multimedia production over a six-month period, bridging pre-school and the first term of compulsory schooling. The upshot of this particular study was that multimedia works comprised only 7.5 per cent of the output of a 4-year-old (taking into account both home and school production), and that all the computer-based work took place at home, largely on the graphic and drawing program KidPix. There are implications for further studies in the home–school dynamic in literacy learning, as 80 per cent of the 266 works created over this six-month period were made at home, with more writing at home than at school and a general difference being that school work was more categorized ('emergent writing', 'handwriting practice', 'seriation' and 'representation', for example), whereas home-based work integrated and moved between different visual and verbal modes of representation.

Cited earlier in this book is the research of Levinovic-Healy (1999), whose study of reading in a post-typographic age includes case studies of two 8-year-old children (one male, one female). An implication of the study concerns the effects on children of 'discontinuities resulting from the predominance of electronically-based reading experiences at home, and the predominance of print reading experiences in school' (abstract). The study is also interesting in that it attempts to describe the different social contexts (specifically, home backgrounds and access to technology) of the two children involved, tracing the impact of access to digital technology on their progress with reading in the classroom. One child ('Sarah') is an expert reader across technologies and modes, while the other ('Warren') is largely indifferent to print and expert in digital media. One of the conclusions of the research is that computers 'are powerfully influential and motivating as a reading site, and [have] the potential to scaffold a reader's textual activities in ways which are not possible in a print context without the presence of human support' (p. 401). Another is that reading has to be conceived as including the decoding and interpretation of still and moving images, both in their own right and in relation to printed verbal texts. The implications for the teaching of reading are considerable.

Digital literacies

I have already indicated earlier in the book that in the new conceptions of literacy (or literacies) the basic encoding of language is digital. Although speech and print are fundamentally different channels through which language is shaped and communicated, the digital encoding enables language to be realized in a number of different formats. Print literacy, in particular, seen for over five hundred years as *the* format for written language, is now seen as one of a number of formats in which language can be presented.

Goodwyn's edited book, *English in the Digital Age* (2000a) takes the idea of digital literacy as a given, but also explores the tensions such a conception creates in the day-to-day practice of English teachers. One aspect of the impact of ICT on English teaching that was perceived to be of relatively low significance in the mid-1990s, according to the Harrison evaluation (1998) and which has not been mentioned much in this chapter, is addressed by Goodwyn in one of his own chapters in the book: that of email. As Goodwyn puts it:

> It is not just the speed and reciprocity of email that enhances learning; it is also the medium itself. It is a new hybrid form of communication that brings speech and writing together, inviting conversational writing with a voice that the reader will soon 'hear'.

It encourages groups to discuss and debate issues that they are interested in; these electronic communities can have long or short lives, inclusive or exclusive membership. In other words, email is a linguistic and symbolic phenomenon, something for students to reflect upon as well as use. (p. 19)

One striking analogy Goodwyn makes is between the virtuality of conventional English work, especially in the use of fiction in classrooms where a possible world (that offered by the novel, say) operates within other framed worlds (those of the classroom, school and curriculum), and the clearly marked virtuality of computer simulations, games and educational software packages. A ground-breaking research project that began in 1999, in a collaboration between Middlesex University's School of Art Design and Performing Arts together with its School of Lifelong Learning and Education and schools in the London Borough of Haringey, saw virtual worlds being at the heart of the project. The Vertex project, still ongoing at the time of writing, sought to explore how children aged 7–11 could navigate virtual spaces and connect such exploration to other curriculum subjects.

In a paper entitled 'Children's Creation of Shared 3D Worlds', Moar and Bailey (2000) write about the Vertex project, stressing how it is based on an art and design tradition of children *making* objects. Being makers rather than just users encourages engagement and transformation, making learning more likely and a richer experience than in the receptive mode. Furthermore, the project's aim was to help children to investigate their own families rather than to indulge in high-technology playing, though the latter dimension was important too. The medium for exploration in this project was the creation of virtual spaces or worlds. As Moar and Bailey note, 'such spaces are related to multi-user chat rooms, in which participants can communicate with each other synchronously, but with the addition of a 3D depiction of the shared environment'. This environment enabled children to 'chat' – in writing – with remote participants (the two actual sites for the work were schools in London and Orkney, northern Scotland), build structures and choose a variety of avatars. Furthermore, children were particularly keen to add voice contact to the repertoire of communicative possibilities.

Collins (2000), in researching the ICT capability of students and beginning teachers in Northern Ireland, found a mismatch between the level of resourcing of ICT in schools – generally thought to be 'good', even if behind that in England – and the levels of confidence and competence among beginning teachers. She suggests that thinking that teaching students will gain command of the ICT skills necessary to affect their English teaching during the twelve weeks at university and twenty-four weeks in practice schools that make up the current postgraduate certificate in education is 'a waste of time' (p. 39). There needs to be much more integration between schools and higher education institutions to effect such progress, and further coordination between the initial stages of teacher education and the continuing professional development of teachers.

Prain and Lyons (2000), in the same volume, discuss the Australian perspective. In a review of research undertaken largely in Australia, and also in England, they note many of the same tensions characterized separately by Goodwyn and Collins, and in addition a disparity between what children and young people bring to the classroom (often fairly or very sophisticated knowledge of ICT application) and the relatively primitive state of the art in schools. Two case studies illuminate their argument, pointing towards the need for new conceptions of the subject, further professional development for teachers and increased emphasis on 'critical literacy' in order to help students to manage, understand and contribute to the communicative maelstrom in which they live. The dimension of critical literacy, often missing from curricula in North America and Europe, is discussed elsewhere in this book (see Morgan, 1997; Levinovic-Healy, 1999).

ICT in English at secondary level

O'Donoghue (2000), a coordinator of English education for 11–14-year-olds, describes a number of ways in which she has used ICT in the teaching of English. First, she discusses the democratic nature of the Web, equating it to books (and thus breaking down barriers that some teachers erect against ICT). Second, she addresses questions of access, noting that 2000 secondary schools in Britain owned an average of one computer per 8.7 students. Third, she draws our attention to the fact that preparing English students for the world – with the 'global citizen' in mind – is an increasingly demanding and necessary act on the part of English teachers. The incorporation of citizenship in the English National Curriculum from 2002 is a reflection of such a need.

In terms of writing, O'Donoghue indicates that writing with ICT involves much more than merely presenting a 'best' version of a finished product. As well as enabling students to make successive drafts and to compose collaboratively more readily than with pen and paper, ICT requires a different attitude to writing. The creation of a website, for instance, requires design and a consideration of the contiguity of the verbal and visual as well as well-honed writing techniques to make the text accessible and inviting to the on-screen reader. Evaluation of these skills as manifested in the final product can take place orally in class and/or online. It makes sense for the IT department in the school to link with English to explore common ground (for example, in the creation of slide shows, commentary upon the research and design process in IT, databases, spreadsheets, websites, intranets and other aspects of communication).

As far as reading goes, O'Donoghue notes that much of what goes for writing applies to reading too; as we have seen earlier in the book, writing and reading are seen as reciprocal activities. Because of the visual dimension to the on-screen interface, reading can be construed as similar to the decoding and interpretation of printed text, but also analogous to 'reading' film and other still and moving visual forms (see Agarwal-Hollands and Andrews, 2001). What we are seeing in reading, however, is an empowerment of the reader to alter, intervene, respond to texts he or she is encountering, so that the whole process of reading and writing approximates speaking and listening. As reading-response theorists of the 1970s and 1980s would have it, readers are *making* the texts.

O'Donoghue is interesting on the way ICT operates in relation to speaking and listening, too, but it is her focus on the Web's capacity for research by students that is the most exciting dimension educationally. Although it is not ground-breaking to extol the virtues of ICT as a research tool, it has to be acknowledged that the medium has transformed the business and possibility of research for students as young as six or seven. There are research methods to learn as well as information to discover via research:

> Research, in the form of browsing, note-taking and bookmarking [will follow identification of a topic and initial searching. Students] will need to note the content, the accessibility, the reading age, the organization and the design of each site, perhaps awarding marks in each category. Ideally, these website guides can be published on the school website or intranet in an appropriate style for others'

use at school and at home, and perhaps updated by teachers in each faculty or department, rather like a university reading list. (O'Donoghue, 2000: 79)

The main drive will be to give students control of the media offered by ICT, rather than be passive users of the technology. Handling the form, as well as the information that it gives us access to, is a critical leap for teachers and students. There is already case-study research (e.g. Barnsley, private correspondence; Abbott, 2000) of websites designed and run by children/students. As O'Donoghue concludes, 'If English teachers can provide the means and the inspiration to enable students to take control, to become enthusiastic, expert and innovative producers, not passive consumers, then we will have gone some way towards providing an English education for the [new] century' (2000: 86).

Of course, it is often teachers rather than students who have to do the catching up. An enlightening chapter by Zancanella, Hall and Pence (2000) records how three English educators in New Mexico put aside their native resistance to computer games and made an effort to play a number of games in order to find out more about them. Throughout, they treated the games 'as literature'; that is to say, they assumed that the games operated via the same rules as printed fiction: you are invited to enter a possible world and respond emotionally, intellectually and morally to its particular challenges. Such acts of imagination soon reveal the differences as well as the similarities between computer games and fiction. Whereas there had been a good deal of research in the 1970s and 1980s on the position of the reader in relation to the emerging fiction (see, for example, Protherough, 1986), the computer games trialled by Zancanella, Hall and Pence (separately) involved the reader/player not only standing at the shoulder of or 'floating above' characters in the fiction, but also taking an active part in the development of the story. Far from being a passive involvement, such proactivity (albeit within confines set by the programmer) might be seen to be *more* educational than the relatively more passive activity of book reading. The significant difference not mentioned by the authors, however, is that ultimately the printed fiction allows imaginative space to the reader in the way that the more immediate tramlines of the interactive computer game does not. The advantages of engaging critically with computer (or 'console') games are worth reciting:

We can help students to understand the immersive, co-creative properties of console games and see them as metaphors for how to approach all texts with a stronger feeling of agency, equipping them with strategies that can make them better readers of their world. And, hopefully, the more circular and ambiguous nature of computer narratives can promote tolerance for ambiguity and difference, and enhance our abilities to live in an increasingly unpredictable and multicultural 'real' world. (Zancanella, Hall and Pence, 2000: 102)

Snyder (1991) is a small-scale study into the impact of computers on students' writing in an Australian secondary school. This study was particularly significant in that it explored whether writing on computer was more effective and more useful with some genres rather than others. The subtitle of the paper is 'A comparative study of the effects of pens and word processors on writing context, process and product'. It describes how the research found that computer-equipped writing classrooms were more student centred, less teacher dominated and more work focused; the atmosphere was more cooperative and collaborative. Students' composing behaviours varied according to the genre and task rather than according to the influence of the writing tool. The investigation of the quality of texts offered 'strong evidence of the efficacy of word processing in improving the quality of writing' in argument and report genres, and weaker evidence for narrative genres. This may be because the writing process in the composition of arguments and reports is more a matter of arranging the building blocks of prose than in the additive, organic flow of narrative composition where 'shaping at the point of utterance' (Britton) is more of a driving force. The facilities offered in wordprocessing programs to arrange and rearrange blocks of text (paragraphs, sections) may be better suited to non-narrative types of writing.

The role of ICT in relation to framing

To borrow the theoretical terminology of McLachlan and Reid (1994), discussed in the last chapter, the particular *frame* in which these contiguities are played out is increasingly that of the monitor, whether a TV monitor or one attached to a computer or phone.[1]

In a paper from the National Council for Educational Technology (Tweddle *et al.*, 1994) – a paper that at the time was assumed to represent one of the cutting edges of thinking about English – various propositions were put forward, along with questions that have a bearing on the issues discussed in the present chapter. The main propositions put forward were that:

- IT is providing an information-rich society for some;
- the culture of IT is global (though unequally accessed);
- IT is generating a collaborative culture;
- the polarities of home/school, teacher/learner and reading/writing are dissolving;
- images, icons and sounds are used alongside and instead of words for constructing and conveying meaning.

One of the many consequences of such a set of propositions and of the changes already taking place is that the distinctions between English/media studies/communication studies/visual studies are being redrawn.

One of the important breakthroughs made by this conception of English is that reading and writing are reciprocal. This is not a new perception. Barthes, with his notion of the 'writerly' text, and reception-theory and reading-response theory, with their reframing of reading as a creative act, has broken down barriers between reading and writing, suggesting that readers 'make' or compose the text as they read it, and that writers are all the time informed by their reading to different degrees. The analogy with 'speaking and listening' makes the reciprocity clear (though the nature of those reciprocities is different), and the irony remains in successive versions of the National Curriculum in English that although 'speaking and listening' are seen as reciprocal, they are afforded a less than equal share of curriculum time than the still separately conceived 'writing' and 'reading'. The true reciprocity of writing and reading is well described in, for example, Jones (1991).

How, then, does the computer screen facilitate the close connection between composition and critical literacy? The simple answer is by allowing the reader/viewer to manipulate texts, change texts, interfere with the sacrosanct nature of texts: to change their shape, to change words within them, to split them up and reformulate them, to write into existing literary works, to join voices with another text, to create split column texts. Thus the 'dialogue' – to borrow a metaphor from speech and listening, and to use the dominant metaphor in discourse studies post-Bakhtin – between writer and reader, between text and writer/reader, is made an active and interactive one.

The interactivity is not only between reader and text (reader, that is, who becomes writer). It is also between collaborating readers. Much of the evidence of the value of computers in the classroom to date has suggested that the conversation that goes on between students as they sit in front of a screen and manipulate/create text is probably the most valuable activity taking place. There is a renewed critical dialogue taking place, and it is about making things with words (and images) and/or interpreting words (and images). The dialogue is also evident in more distant types of collaboration between readers and writers that technology enables, such as emails in response to questions and messages on the Net. The making and remaking of words and images on the computer screen seems to link with postmodernist ideas about intertextuality and re-presentation.

Literacy in a 'digital' world

The suggestion that we now live in a digital world has been somewhat over-hyped. In 'What's Next for Text?', Lanham (2001) proposes that all text is, at source, digital, and that it can take a number of forms according to medium and purpose. While this notion is undoubtedly true for the vast majority of texts that we produce and read (as long as you include handwriting as somehow 'digitally' analysable and scannable), we must not forget that a mark in the sand with a stick, or graffiti on a wall or passing train count as part of the graphic, written world. Like Andy Goldsworthy art works, they are photographable and thus potentially digital and able to be disseminated.

The truth of the notion that text is digital, however, has implications for the teaching of English. It marks a shift from a set of assumptions which place the book at the heart of English teaching. The logic used to go like this: print on a page is the *locus* of literacy and of the subject, English. The book is the principal cultural form in which print is found. The irreducible mode of writing which takes the book as its expression is fiction. Therefore fiction is at the heart of the subject, English. If, on the other hand, you take the digital to be the irreducible core of text, the logic takes a different route: the alphabet is the code in which many Western languages are written. All texts, however long or short, fictive or non-fictive, are composed of letters. These texts are digital, at source. Therefore they can take a number of forms: book, electronic text, projected panels on a screen, and so on. The shape and form of the texts is a matter of rhetoric – the fitting of a text to its context and its audience. Hence the phrase 'digital rhetorics' to denote the field of what we used to call 'English studies'.

The most significant recent research into digital rhetorics has been in Australia, where a report on a project entitled 'Digital Rhetorics: Literacies and Technologies in Education – Current Practices and Future Directions' was published in 1997 (Lankshear *et al.*, 1997). One of the books emerging from the research is *Teachers and Techno-Literacy: managing literacy, technology and learning in schools* (Lankshear and Snyder, 2000). The key argument of the book is that, in opposition to reductionist and mechanistic views of literacy and learning, 'education must enable learners to become proficient with what we call the "operational", "cultural" and "critical" dimensions of literacy and technology' (p. xvii):

> Becoming proficient with the 'operational', 'cultural' and 'critical' dimensions includes understanding how contemporary economic, social, technological, administrative, organizational and political changes are affecting the social practices of literacy, technology and learning. It also includes understanding how these changes are altering literacy, technology and learning and the relations between them. Further, it incorporates understanding how current changes are placing new 'premiums' on literacy, technology and learning – raising them to new heights of urgency. Most importantly, becoming adept with the 'operational', 'cultural' and 'critical' dimensions suggests ways in which teachers may be able to respond effectively to the new demands associated with technology use. (p. xvii)

The book includes a number of case studies of technology in use in the service of literacy teaching and learning in primary and secondary schools in Australia. In one primary school, a teacher helps 10–11-year-olds to be independent, self-directed and cooperative learners, speaking of her 'commitment to developing students' future lives as evolving technologies promote lifelong learning. She speaks of her commitment to developing students' advanced reading strategies, such as skimming and scanning. [She] places great importance on information skills. She describes literacy as more than reading and writing – students need explicit instruction in new information technologies.' (Lankshear and Snyder, 2000: 99) Consequently, students in this teacher's class, in working on a project on the environment, have a choice over the final form of presentation:

Some are producing fully illustrated folders in the shapes of various Australian fauna, one is producing a concertina-like display board which folds into the shape of a flying fox . . . Others are producing multimedia presentation, using KidPix and ClarisWorks slide shows. Most written work is word-processed. (p. 101)

At secondary level, further examples of practice are described. Some of these are what we now take to be fairly standard practice in the classroom, such as students working together on a keyboard to produce a play-script for performance, research presented in multimedia form, students collaborating on a four-page newspaper or magazine. More innovative examples include cooperation on the making of a HyperCard presentation for a school open day, emailing partner schools, the writing of an electronic novel in collaboration with other schools facilitated by a writer-in-residence, and the creation of websites for business entrepreneurship or for more personal uses.

Interestingly, one of the outcomes of the 'Digital Rhetorics' research is the establishment of five principles to guide the effective integration of the new technologies into classroom-based literacy education and to guide curriculum activity more generally. These are:

- teachers first;
- complementarity;
- workability;
- equity;
- focus on trajectories.

In terms of implications for English teachers at primary and secondary levels, these distil into a need for continuing professional development in the application of the new technologies to the subject – not only, for instance, as part of government-funded schemes for the training of teachers in ICT, but also as part of a longer-term understanding of the need for teachers to keep abreast of new developments and new conceptions of their subject; complementarity in the sense of understanding how ICTs affect conventional practice, how they may be integrated with conventional writing practices and how they may change the landscape of practice in the classroom, especially in relation to home learning; workability in terms of sensible solutions to learning needs in a school, rather than technology-driven purchasing that creates imbalances in the learning community of the school; equity in the sense of making sure that English teachers and students get equal access to computer equipment and software with other curriculum areas, and that it is not assumed that because English is a 'low-technology' subject (as opposed to, say, Science), it does not need considerable resource to ensure that its students are ICT literate. Finally, the emphasis on trajectories implies that English work in schools will have in mind the kind of discourses used in the real world, not only to create simulations of these in the classroom but also to exchange communication with the world beyond school and to equip students to operate confidently with the discourses of that world (or those worlds).

Research in practice, carried out over a number of years in the business of teaching and collaborating on programmes with elementary and high schools as well as in out-of-school workshops and in higher education, is the basis of a book by Kathleen Tyner, *Literacy in a Digital World* (1998). This book locates the debate about ICT and literacy with a wider notion of visual, information and media literacies (literacies which are explored in Chapters 1 and 6 in the present book). The ability to decode information in a variety of forms is, according to Tyner,

> Analogous to the reading of print, but also applicable to audio, graphics and the moving image, a process that Paolo Freire and Donaldo Macedo (1987) call 'reading the world'. If citizens can also manipulate and understand the processes to create messages and distribute them, that is, 'writing the world', then literacy practices accrue maximum benefit to the individual. It would be false to say that this vision of literacy would automatically translate into an equal distribution of social power. It is obvious that those who control both the channels of distribution and the skilful production of compatible content have access to the most favorable opportunities to influence social policy through sustained creative effort. Nonetheless, a sophisticated and powerful vision of literacy shows potential to enable each person to at least join the debate by skillfully negotiating within the existing power structure, as well as outside it. And this is why it is urgent that everyone has access to literacy in its most powerful forms. (p. 4)

One of the many interesting outcomes of Tyner's research is a frustration with the fact that the literatures and theories of information literacy, visual literacy and media literacy 'do not join forces to link their research and findings' (p. 6). There is the need and likelihood of synthesis or integration of these fields in the near future, and curriculum practices will have to change as a result. A joint statement by Mark Reid of the British Film Institute and myself, included in Andrews (2000), might point the way forward for the communication curriculum from the mid-decade onwards. But as Tyner says, it is probably too early to suggest a nomenclature for this new conception. In purely descriptive terms, digital rhetorics of the new literacies come closest to embracing the range of literacies set out above – and thus the potential classroom practices that might emerge from (or drive) the new conception of the field. Yet another important implication of Tyner's work arises from her suggestion that, 'although digital media is currently dominated by the uses of alphabetic literacy on networked computers . . . it is only a matter of time before the moving image becomes equally prolific in digital media' (p. 8).

Finally, Tyner is clear that her work stands in a tradition that has become increasingly aware, since the 1960s, of the bifurcation between the literacy practices of compulsory schooling 'and those that occur outside the schoolhouse door' (p. 8):

> The literacy of schooling, based on a hierarchical access to print literacy, is increasingly at odds with the kinds of constructivist practices necessary to accommodate the more diverse, interactive, and less linear media forms made available by digital technologies. In the absence of strong theory, literacy practices are splitting into the kind of literacy practiced at school and the kind practiced in the *real* world of home and community. (pp. 8–9)

Implications for practice

The implications arising from the ubiquity of the computer and other ICTs for the teaching of English are, perhaps, of all the developments in research discussed in this book, the greatest. The question is not so much one of research about the use of computers in the classroom affecting the teaching and learning of English. Rather, the research and development that has gone into the development of ICTs over the last twenty-five years has far-reaching implications for the future of communication – and, therefore, for the teaching of English.

Some commentators have suggested that the advent of ICTs in the classroom has not yet had a radical effect on the nature of schooling;

and that a time-traveller from the nineteenth century would have no trouble in recognizing that he/she was in an educational setting when landing in a school of today. But things will change. It is possible to imagine that in a few years' time the *use* of schools will change, thus changing the institutional framework within which formal learning takes place (and, consequently, the nature of English as a subject). For example, one scenario is that formal schooling will be concentrated in (say) the morning, when young people are generally at their most focused and alert. A formal, highly regulated and accountable curriculum will be in place, with concentration on the core subjects of English, Maths and Science. The afternoons could be devoted to a wider range of subjects with more choice and more flexibility in delivery and outcome. Subjects such as personal, social and health education, the arts, sport, citizenship, community studies, economics, modern foreign languages and so on could be given timetable space of varying lengths. The evenings could be devoted to lifelong learning sessions for the community. The role of ICT in the re-formation of the school day, and in the function of learning at school as opposed to at home and elsewhere, is considerable.

More immediately, the implications of ICT for English and literacy teaching are:

- a reorientation on the part of teachers in English and all subjects towards an understanding and appreciation of the digital nature of text, and a resultant separation of the notions of 'books' and 'literacy';
- recognition that if text is digital and can be manipulated on screen, it can take various other forms too, all generated from a core digital source;
- continued exploitation of the oral dimension to working with computers: the approximation of email to speech; use of voice recognition software; talk generated by the collaborative use of computers;
- an opening up of the interface between the visual and verbal, with exploration of the history of such contiguity (illuminated manuscripts, children's books, art that contains words and text that is accompanied by illustration, etc.);
- the movement towards a notion of composing as design;
- oscillation between on-screen editing and paper-based editing (e.g. on printouts) in the drafting process;

- incorporation of different genres and text-types into hybrid forms of writing (e.g. the inclusion of tables and graphics in written text), and the creation of new forms of writing;
- increased experimentation with the presentation of writing;
- increasing use of the Internet for research purposes.

Note

1 Howard Hollands has suggested to me the following in relation to the role of computers in art education: 'Communicating in front of a screen and manipulating images and texts must be about something. What is it about? Colour on a TV monitor is not the same as colour in the visually experienced world, although clearly, it is part of that world. The complexities of reflected colour and all those qualities of the outside world can only be recreated on the screen. Chance itself has to be programmed. Perhaps we now enter the spiritual domain of IT. The monitor is just a box of tricks *and* a valid art form, but the form is running way ahead of development in content.'

Chapter 8

Conclusions

Although I have attempted to draw out implications for practice in each of the chapters in the book, there are more general points to make in a concluding chapter with regard to implications for language education policy and for future research in the field. This chapter therefore is not so much a summary of what has appeared in the book as a look forward to policy and practice in the light of research findings to date.

The first point must be a caveat, however. Research *findings* is a loose term. Strictly speaking, we should be looking for *results* from research projects which can provide us with a firm foundation on which to build. Findings provide a less secure foundation, as they are more open to interpretation and (usually) more tentative. Some research analysts would say that *findings* are usually the outcome of qualitative research which manifest themselves in the imprecisions of language and supposition, whereas *results* are the outcome of hypotheses which are tested and which produce black-and-white answers. To make such a dichotomy of the qualitative/quantitative spectrum is, however, to over-simplify the picture. The question of whether a research project provides findings or results is more a matter of the balance between the hypothesis or question on the one hand, and the proof/disproof or answer(s) on the other. In other words, the hypothesis or question has to be clearly framed for there to be clear results. Equally, the proof/disproof of the hypothesis or the answer(s) to the question(s) has to be conclusive. If there is any lack of clarity in the formulation of either side of the equation (whatever the nature of the equation), we are likely to get findings. If there is more precision in the design of the equation, we will get results.

There is one further general point by way of preface to this last chapter. All research, however conclusive, requires further research, because of the inquisitive nature of learning. Hypotheses may be proved or disproved, and questions may be answered, but the very nature of the conclusions will bring forth new hypotheses and questions.

Accepting these general points, what are the particular implications for language education policy and for further research in the field that arise from the critical survey undertaken in this book?

The nature and scope of English

In the first chapter, the nature of English was considered. What emerged in the late 1980s and in the 1990s was that the subject English, in schools at least, had formed itself around notions of what one could say *about* language and language use. This position already looks dated. Knowing about language is one thing; but using it, making it and critiquing it are likely to be more essential features of the use of language in the first years of the present century. As communication becomes more ubiquitous and more frequent, and as a result communication management becomes more and more an essential ingredient of practice at home and at work, the emphasis on creative and critical literacy increases. No longer is it possible to be a passive user of the language without immersing oneself in consumerism and thus being prey to the whims of corporate hegemony. The active user of language, however, helps to fashion the worlds in which he/she operates. Critical literacy, it seems to me, helped us to see that reading against the text – or at least, being resistant to the ideologies that often worked surreptitiously within texts – was a first and necessary step to becoming an informed and intelligent reader and citizen. The next step is to become a more creative maker of language and manager of communication. What research has shown is that a learner who is in passive mode is less likely to develop as a language user than someone who is prepared to fashion it for him- or herself.

Another major point to emerge from the study of the nature and function of English is that the term 'English', as used to describe a loosely defined subject and discipline in schools and universities, is rapidly becoming inappropriate. 'English' may denote the language used (as opposed to French or Hindi) but it cannot for much longer be used to denote the wider programme of study that includes literatures from different countries and cultures; moving image studies; visual literacies;

translations from one language to another; and studies in semiotics. The more accurate technical term is rhetoric, in the most positive sense of that word. If we take rhetoric to be the 'arts of discourse', we have a sufficiently broad but equally rigorous definition and practice within which to work. One of the many advantages of such a formulation is that it is language independent. That is to say, rhetoric can operate in whichever context it finds itself in and with whatever languages (verbal, mathematical, musical) it encounters. It removes the cultural association of 'English' with England and 'Englishness'. Pragmatically, however, it may be best to continue with the present term, however imperfect and inappropriate it is.

The changing relationship of research, policy and practice

If we think of the relationship between research, policy and practice in terms of a triangle, it is clear that we are still some way from an equilateral triangle in the field of education. In this respect, education lags behind health and medicine, where there are well-established centres – at least in the UK, but probably elsewhere too – which provide critical and systematic reviews of research for policy and practice. In England, the National Health Service's Reviews and Dissemination Centre at the University of York provides just such a service for the health community. The Cochrane Library in Oxford collects, filters and presents summaries of research for a wide audience in health and medicine, and the Campbell group performs a similar role for health, social sciences and other audiences. In the education field, the DfEE initiated in the winter of 1999/2000 an Evidence-Informed Policy and Practice Initiative (EPPI) in education in the Social Science Research Unit of the Institute of Education, London. The plan of the centre is to set up panels in up to fifty different areas of education and to review education research in these areas against systematically generated criteria for quality in research. The present series, Continuum Studies in Research in Education, is the beginning of Continuum's contribution to such an enterprise.

The introduction to the series as a whole suggests that until policy, practice and research come into a more balanced relationship – preferably an equilibrium – then practice is likely to continue without regard to research. Equally, policy and research, in their own ways, will continue without due regard for practice. The aim of this book has been to bring research and practice, at least, into closer proximity.

Many of the implications for research have been drawn out or pointed out in the individual chapters. In more general terms, perhaps the first ingredient for successful transition from research into practice is that teachers must be engaged in the process of undertaking or understanding research. The best of these approaches is the actual undertaking of new research, involving as it always does the consideration of previous research. Action or practitioner research has been described in the series introduction, and readers wishing to know more should consult, for example, Webb (1990), Webb and Vulliamy (1992) and others. But second best – the reading, interpreting and understanding of research – is a very good second and it has been the intention of this book to make such connections possible.

The challenge of ICTs to conventional notions of literacy

Extensive references to Lankshear and Snyder's (2000) distillation of some of the issues arising from the Australian Digital Literacies project in the previous chapter point the way to further research for English and language education. I will set out the implications for policy of recent developments at the interface of technology, literacy and learning, and then begin to chart areas for further research.

There is a tension in many governments' thinking about policies for literacy and language education. On the one hand, governments seem excited by the promises of new technologies and see them almost as panaceas for educational problems. On the other, governments like to control the nature of literacy, resorting to older, narrower conceptions against which children's progress can be measured. There is a further tension in that governments have inherited an essentially nineteenth-century model of schooling against which the new technologies pose interesting and seemingly insurmountable problems.

Why is it that governments espouse so wholeheartedly the new technologies' potential for educational transformation? Is it because they, like smaller organizations and individuals, are caught up in a frenzy of excitement at the potential of ICTs to change communication and management practices? Is it that they fear being left behind in the global communications revolution when it comes to economic advantage? Or is it more likely that they have considered the available research on the impact of ICTs on learning, and are making rational decisions about the future shape of policy as a result? History would suggest that, in the last twenty years of development of computers in classrooms, there is little rationality at play. The stronger influence is one based on conviction rather than considered planning, with technical innovation running faster than pedagogical application – and certainly faster than evaluation or research can keep up.

When placed alongside an increasing emphasis on assessment in school curricula (at increasingly frequent intervals in a child's development, at least in England and Wales), a picture is emerging of communication by writing being more prevalent again than communication by speaking and listening. In the period from about 1980 to about 1995, speech seemed to be gaining ascendancy in the curriculum, with refined methods of assessment giving it the status in the school curriculum that it had lacked for many decades. But that ascendancy seems to have waned again in the light of the ubiquity of email and the emphasis on 'pencil and paper' tests of progress and attainment. A further factor in its (temporary?) demise is the governmental insistence on whole-class teaching methods – which fall into the transmission mode of education delivery. Such methods give less space for small group discussion, and thus sacrifice speaking and listening to a less interactive, more passive form of learning.

Research, therefore, is needed to track such changes and to determine whether present methods of teaching and learning, and present curriculum formulations, are likely to bear fruit. Specifically, questions which need further research as far as speaking and listening go include the following:

- What are the benefits that ICTs can bring to the improvement of speaking and listening in the classroom?
- Is the balance between speaking and listening in the curriculum an appropriate one?
- Do voice recognition technologies have a place in the learning of writing?
- What benefits are there for children with special needs with regard to speaking and listening?

The last question leads us on to the question of reading, reading development and difficulties with reading. We have seen in the chapter on reading that attempts have already been made to use ICTs in the service of helping dyslexic readers to solve or ameliorate their problems.

Further research is needed in this area, but such technology-induced research should not disguise the fact that research is still needed on the processes of reading. Major advances have been made over the past thirty years, but the following questions remain:

- Now that we know that learning to read is a complex matter of operating systematically at the various levels of language, and also being able to integrate those levels to construct meaning from print, what do we know about the processes of such integration?
- Is the model for learning to read print appropriate for studies in how young people learn to read on-screen?
- What is the proper balance for studies in reading development? Should it take the grapho-phonemic levels as essential to the business of learning to read, or should other levels gain more prominence (and more research into their modes of operation)?
- What is the role of the visual in learning to read?

It has been asserted in the course of the book that reading and writing are as reciprocal as speaking and listening. If this is the case, further studies are required in the field of writing:

- Is the model of compositional and secretarial skills a suitable one to take forward into the twenty-first century? If not, what alternative models are there?
- Is the practice of drafting and redrafting at deep and surface levels still appropriate for classroom use?
- Does redrafting suit some kinds of writing better than others?
- What are the implications of the notion of 'shaping at the point of utterance' for compositional practice?
- What new genres and text types are required for the next decade?
- Must school genres of writing continue to be so different from genres in the real world?
- Are the meta-genres of narrative, argument and description still appropriate for schooling?
- What impact do spelling and grammar checkers have on the capability to spell and to write language effectively and accurately?

Questions such as those outlined above in relation to speaking, listening, reading and writing beg the larger question, namely to what extent is policy – and particularly the formation of curriculum and assessment policy and practice – keeping up with research and practice in the classroom? Perhaps the key issue for policy-makers, software and hardware developers, researchers and teachers to consider is whether the currently conceived narrow definitions of literacy are actually a disservice to young people. Wider conceptions of literacy, which consider the contexts of literacy, multiple literacies, multilingual literacies and multimodal literacies are more pertinent to life and work in the near future, and should therefore inform the curriculum and its assessment. Those wider conceptions of literacy have been discussed in Chapters 1 and 7.

As far as the balance between literature and the moving image is concerned, we are possibly looking at a false dichotomy. But whereas the moving image, to a large extent, has been employed in the service of literature ('the film of the text'), policy will have to take account of the increasing pressure to recognize the centrality of the moving image to young people's lives and education. The BFI report, *Making Movies Matter* (Bazalgette *et al.*, 1999), discussed in Chapter 6, sets the template for the future of art works in visual and verbal languages. As ever, further questions remain to be answered with regard to literature and still and moving image education, including:

- What version of visual literacy will be needed by young people in ten years' time?
- How will the verbal and the visual sit alongside each other in a new theory of discourse?
- What impact will moving image education have on the curriculum as a whole, and particularly on 'English'?
- Are notions of a canon of literature and/or film untenable in the twenty-first century? If not, what is to be the canon for school curricula?
- What further practical moves are necessary for moving image education to be more centrally established in classroom practice?
- What pedagogies of literature and/or still and moving image education need to be developed?

Finally, though ICTs might be seen to be the catalyst of many of the changes that have happened to school education over the last twenty years, and in particular to the English and language curriculum, it is clear from the questions outlined above that not all future research is going to be driven by technological change. Perhaps the biggest question of them all for the future of schooling is whether it will be necessary or desirable, in ten to fifteen years' time, for young people to attend school in order to develop language capabilities in the widest sense. The demise of schooling itself has long been predicted. Such absolutism is unlikely to occur in practice, with a more likely outcome being the change in the school day within existing school premises.

In the shorter term, questions still remain unanswered about the impact of ICTs in the English curriculum. These include:

- What are the implications of multimedia for literacy development and the design of literacy programmes?
- Is it necessary to learn the codes of the printed written system before embarking on design issues in multimedia?
- Is design the new framing activity for English?
- What are the implications of wireless application protocol technology for communications between young people, and between young people and banks and archives of information?
- How will the higher conceptual demands of argumentation and other forms of rationality cope in the face of increased access to information?
- What issues of access continue to make for inequalities within society?
- How can current and new technologies best be harnessed in the service of education in the language arts?

It is these and other questions which will continue to exercise researchers, teachers and others involved in the development of language education over the coming years. What this book has tried to do is build on the research undertaken in the last thirty or so years to provide a solid foundation upon which practitioners and policy-makers might build better practice and better policy. The aim of such improvement is to make learning more engaging, more effective and more creative, thus contributing to young people's self-esteem and personal, social and political development. The enhancement of language education, in all its forms, is central to that enterprise.

Bibliography

Abbott, C. (2000) *Some Young Male Website Owners: the technological aesthete, the community builder and the political activist*. British Film Institute invitation seminar, Coventry: BECTa.

Abbs, P. (1976) *Root and Blossom: essays on the philosophy, practice and politics of English teaching*. London: Heinemann Educational.

Abbs, P. (1982) *English within the Arts: a radical alternative for English and the arts in the curriculum*. London: Hodder and Stoughton.

Abbs, P. (ed.) (1987) *Living Powers: the arts in education*. London: Falmer.

Agarwal-Hollands, U. and Andrews, R. (2001) 'From Scroll to Codex . . . and Back Again', *Education, Communication & Information* 1(1).

Ali, S. (1995) 'Teaching Literature in English in a Malaysian ESL Context: reflections and recommendations', *English in Education* 29(1): 53–65.

Allen, D. (1994) 'Teaching Visual Literacy – some reflections on the term', *Journal of Art and Design Education* 13(2): 133–43.

Anderson, H. (1995) 'Monsterous Plans? Standard English in the National Curriculum and Norwegian in the Monsterplan', *English in Education* 29(1): 14–19.

Anderson, H. and Hilton, M. (1997) 'Speaking Subjects: the development of a conceptual framework for the teaching and learning of spoken language', *English in Education* 31(1): 12–23.

Andrews, R. (1981) 'Telling Stories', *The English Magazine* 7(Summer), 21–5.

Andrews, R. (ed.) (1989) *Narrative and Argument*. Milton Keynes: Open University Press.

Andrews, R. (1991) *The Problem with Poetry*. Milton Keynes: Open University Press.

Andrews, R. (1992a) 'An Investigation into Narrative and Argumentative Structures in the Writing of Year 8 Students', *School of Education*. Hull: University of Hull.

Andrews, R. (ed.) (1992b) *Rebirth of Rhetoric: essays in language, culture, education*. London: Routledge.

Andrews, R. (1995) *Teaching and Learning Argument*. London: Cassell.

Andrews, R. (1996a) 'Editorial', *English in Education: international perspectives on English* **29**(1): 1–3.

Andrews, R. (ed.) (1996b) *Interpreting the New National Curriculum*. London: Middlesex University Press.

Andrews, R. (1996c) 'Visual Literacy in Question', *20:20* **4**(June): 17–20.

Andrews, R. (1997a) 'Editorial: electronic english', *English in Education* **31**(2): 1–3.

Andrews, R. (ed.) (1997b) *English in Education: special issue on electronic English*. Sheffield: National Association for the Teaching of English.

Andrews, R. (1997c) 'Reconceiving Argument', *Educational Review* **49**(3): 259–69.

Andrews, R. (1998a) 'Image, Text, Persuasion: the case of a four-year-old's graphic production', in C. Woods (ed.), *Image, Text and Persuasion*. Adelaide: University of South Australia: Centre for Professional and Public Communication, pp. 7–27.

Andrews, R. (1998b) 'The Nature of "Visual Literacy": problems and possibilities for the classroom', *Literacy Learning: Secondary Thoughts* **6**(2): 8–16.

Andrews, R. (2000a) 'Framing and Design in ICT in English: towards a new subject and new practices in the classroom', in A. Goodwyn (ed.), *English in the Digital Age*. London: Cassell, pp. 22–33.

Andrews, R. (2000b) *Learning, Literacy and ICT: what's the connection?* Paper presented at *Raising the achievement of secondary pupils through literacy and ICT in every curriculum subject*. London: Middlesex University.

Andrews, R., Ashdown, P., McGuinn, N. and Hakes, B. (1994) 'Opening New Worlds: an international literature project'. Hull: University of Hull.

Andrews, R. and Clarke, S. (1996) 'Information Technology, Information and the English Curriculum', *The English and Media Magazine* **35**(November): 35–9.

Andrews, R., Clarke, S. and Costello, P. J. M. (1993) 'Improving the Quality of Argument'. Hull: University of Hull: School of Education, Centre for Studies in Rhetoric.

Andrews, R. and Fisher, A. (1991) *Narratives*. Cambridge: Cambridge University Press.

Andrews, R. and Mitchell, S. (2001) *Essays in Argument*. London: Middlesex University Press.

Andrews, R. and Simons, M. (1996) 'The Electronic Word: multimedia, rhetoric and English teaching', *The English and Media Magazine* **35**(November): 40–3.

Appleyard, B. (1990) *Becoming a Reader*. Cambridge: Cambridge University Press.

APU (1982) Assessment of Performance Unit, *Primary Survey*. London: APU.

Arnold, R. (1991) *Writing Development*. Milton Keynes: Open University Press.

Ashton, E. (1994) 'Metaphor in Context: an examination of the significance of metaphor for reflection and communication', *Educational Studies* **20**(3): 357–66.

Ashton, E. (1997) 'Extending the Scope of Metaphor: an examination of definitions old and new and their significance for education', *Educational Studies* **23**(2): 195–214.

Assessment of Performance Unit (1982) *Language Performance in Schools: Primary Survey Report No. 1*. London: Her Majesty's Stationery Office.

Bakhtin, M. M. (1981) *The Dialogic Imagination*. Austin, TX: University of Texas Press.

Baldick, C. (1983) *The Social Mission of English Criticism 1848–1932*. Oxford: Clarendon Press.

Barnes, A. (1993) 'Key Stages in the Development of Key Stage 3 SATs', *English in Education* **27**(1): 4–9.

Barnes, D., Britton, J. and Rosen, H. (1969) *Language, the Learner and the School*. Harmondsworth: Pelican.

Barnes, D., Britton, J. and Rosen, H. (1971) *Language, the Learner and the School*. London: Pelican.

Barnes, D., Britton, J. and Torbe, M. (1986) *Language, the Learner and the School*. London: Pelican.

Barnett, M. (1994) *Paper on Technological Literacy*. Domains of Literacy, London: Institute of Education.

Barratt, A. J. B. (1998) *Audit of Media in English*. London: British Film Institute.

Bateson, G. (1954) 'A Theory of Play and Fantasy', *Steps to an Ecology of Mind*. New York: Ballantine.

Bazalgette, C. *et al.* (1997) *Backtracks*. London: British Film Institute.

Bazalgette, C. *et al.* (1999) *Making Movies Matter: report of the Film Education Working Group*. London: British Film Institute.

Bazerman, C. (1988) *Shaping Written Knowledge: the genres and activity of the experimental article in Science*. Madison, WI: University of Wisconsin Press.

Bazerman, C. (1994) 'Where is the Classroom?', in A. Freedman and P. Medway (eds), *Learning and Teaching Genre*. Portsmouth, NH: Heinemann/Boynton-Cook.

Beard, R. (ed.) (1993) *Teaching Literacy: balancing perspectives*. London: Hodder and Stoughton.

Beavis, C. (1995) '"This Special Place": literature in senior forms in the 1990s', *English in Education* **29**(1): 20–7.

Benton, M. (1984) 'The Methodology Vacuum in Teaching Literature', *Language Arts* **61**(3).

Benton, M. (2000) *Studies in the Spectator Role: literature, painting and pedagogy*. London: Routledge and Falmer.

Benton, M. and Fox, G. (1985) *Teaching Literature 9–14*. London: Oxford University Press.

Benton, M., Teasey, J., Bell, R. and Hurst, K. (1988) *Young Readers Responding to Poems*. London: Routledge.

Bergonzi, B. (1990) *Exploding English: criticism, theory, culture*. Oxford: Clarendon Press.

Bernstein, B. (1971) *Class, Codes and Control*. London: Routledge & Kegan Paul.

Bernstein, B. (1972) 'Social Class, Language and Socialization', in A. Cashdan *et al.* (eds), *Language in Education: a source book*. London: Routledge & Kegan Paul in association with the Open University, pp. 102–10.

BFI (1997) *Backtracks*. London: British Film Institute.

Black, M. (1971) 'Models and Metaphors', in I. T. Ramsey (ed.), *Words about God*. London: SCM Press, pp. 177–80.

Bousted, M. (1993) 'When Will They Ever Learn? the influence of the Centre for Policy Studies upon government education policy', *English in Education* **27**(3): 33ff.

Boyle, M. (1998) 'Storytelling, Relevance and the Bilingual Child', *English in Education* **32**(2): 15–23.

Brake, J. (1996) *Changing Images: photography, education and young people*. Salford: Viewpoint Photography Gallery.

Brindley, S. (ed.) (1994) *Teaching English*. London: Routledge.

Britton, J., Burgess, T., Martin, N., McLeod, A. and Rosen, H. (1975) *The Development of Writing Abilities 11–18 (Schools Council Project on the Written Language of 11–18-year-olds)*. London: Macmillan.

Brooks, G., Foxman, G. and Gorman, T. (1995) 'Standards in Literacy and Numeracy 1948–1994'. London: National Commission on Education.

Brown, D., Martino, W., Rijlaarsdan, G., D'Antonio Stinson, A. and Whiting, M. (2000) 'Annotated Bibliography of Research in the Teaching of English', *Research in the Teaching of English* **34**(4): 566–73.

Brown, J., Clarke, S., Medway, P., Stibbs, A. with Andrews, R. (1990) 'Developing English for TVEI (the DEFT Report)'. Leeds: University of Leeds/The Training Agency.

Brown, J. I. (1949) 'The Construction of a Diagnostic Test of Listening Comprehension', *Journal of Experimental Education* **18**: 139–46.

Brown, J. I. and Carlesen, G. R. (1953) 'Brown-Carlesen Listening Comprehension Test, grades 9–13'. Yonkers, NY: World Book Co.

Bruner, J. (1986) *Actual Minds, Possible Worlds*. Cambridge MA: Harvard University Press.

Bryan, B. (1995) 'The Role of Context in Defining Adolescent Responses to Poetry: a comparative case', *English in Education* **29**(1): 42–9.

Bullock, A. (1975) 'A Language for Life: the Bullock Report'. London: Her Majesty's Stationery Office/Department of Education and Science.

Cameron, D. and Low, G. (1999) 'Metaphor', *Language Teaching* **32**(2): 77–96.

Carroll, D. (1987) *Paraesthetics: Foucault, Lyotard, Derrida*. New York: Methuen.

Cazden, C. *et al.* (1996) 'A Pedagogy of Multiliteracies: designing social futures', *Harvard Educational Review* **66**(1): 60–92.

Chandran, N. (1995) 'Using Reading Frames: an example from "The Waste Land"', *English in Education* **29**(1): 31–9.

Chomsky, N. (1964) *Syntactic Structures*. Cambridge, MA: MIT Press.

Chomsky, N. (1965) *Aspects of the Theory of Syntax*. Cambridge, MA: MIT Press.

Clark, U. (1994) 'Bring English to Order: a personal account of the National Curriculum Council English evaluation project', *English in Education* **28**(1): 33ff.

Clarke, S. (2000) 'Changing Technology, Changing Shakespeare, or Our Daughter is a Misprint', in A. Goodwyn (ed.), *English in the Digital Age*. London: Cassell, pp. 103–14.

Clarke, S. and Sinker, J. (1991) *Arguments*. Cambridge: Cambridge University Press.

Cliff Hodges, G., Moss, J. and Shreeve, A. (2000) 'The Future of English', *English in Education* **34**(1): 1–11.

Coles, M. and Jenkins, R. (1998) *Assessing Reading 2: Changing Practice in Classrooms: international perspectives on reading assessment*. London: Routledge.

Collins, F. (1996) 'Telling Tales – Finding the Words: what do storytellers say about children and stories?', *English in Education* 30(3): 38–47.

Collins, J. (2000) 'ICT in English: views from Northern Ireland', in A. Goodwyn (ed.), *English in the Digital Age*. London: Cassell, pp. 34–52.

Conteh, J. (1993) 'Unrecognized Assets: linguistic diversity in the mainstream primary classroom', *English in Education* 27(1): 46–53.

Costello, P. J. M. and Mitchell, S. (1995) *Competing and Consensual Voices: the theory and practice of argument*. Clevedon, Bristol: Multilingual Matters.

Cox, B. (1989) *English for Ages 5–16*. London: Department of Education and Science.

Darby, R., Dawes, L., Dennison, A., Gallagher, C., Loomes, W., Reid, H. and Stanton, J. (1997) 'Reading on Screen: exploring issues in reading for information with CDRom', *English in Education* 31(2): 34–44.

Dasenbrock, R. W. (1992) 'Teaching Multicultural Literature', in J. A. W. Trimmer (ed.), *Understanding Others*. Urbana, Illinois: National Council of Teachers of English, pp. 35–46.

Davies, C. (1996) *What is English Teaching?* Buckingham: Open University Press.

Daw, P. (1996) 'Achieving Higher Grades at A Level English Literature: an investigation into the factors that contribute to schools' successes', *English in Education* 30(3): 15–27.

Daw, P., Smith, J. and Wilkinson, S. (1997) 'Factors Associated with High Standards in Spelling in Years R–4', *English in Education* 31(1): 36–47.

Delamont, S. (1990) *Sex Roles and the School*. London: Methuen.

Department of Education and Science (DES) (1966) *Progress in Reading 1948–1964*: education pamphlet no. 50. London: Her Majesty's Stationery Office.

Department of Education and Science (DES) (1972) *Children with Specific Reading Difficulties*. London: Her Majesty's Stationery Office.

DfEE (1999a) *The National Curriculum for England*. London: Department for Education and Employment/Qualifications and Curriculum Authority.

DfEE (1999b) *English: The National Curriculum for England Key Stages 1–4*. London: Department for Education and Employment and Qualifications and Curriculum Authority.

DfEE (1998) *Teachers: Meeting the Challenge of Change*. London: HMSO.

DfEE (2000) *Professional Development*. London: Department for Education and Employment.

Dixon, J. (1991) *A Schooling in 'English': critical episodes in the struggle to shape literary and cultural studies*. Buckingham: Open University Press.

Dixon, J. (1994) 'Categories to Frame an English Curriculum?', *English in Education* 28(1): 3ff.

Dixon, J. and Stratta, L. (1982) 'Argument: what does it mean to teachers of English?', *English in Education* 16(1): 41–54.

Donaldson, M. (1977) 'The Prediction of Ability', in J. F. D. Reid (ed.), *Reading: problems and practices*. London: Ward Lock Educational, pp. 13–19.

Doyle, B. (1989) *English and Englishness*. London: Routledge.

Eagleton, T. (1983) *Literary Theory*. Oxford: Blackwell.

Eisner, E. (1989) 'Structure and Magic in Discipline-based Art Education', in D. Thistlewood (ed.), *Critical Studies in Art and Design Education*. Harlow: Longman.

Emig, J. (1971) *The Composing Processes of Twelfth Graders*. Urbana, Illinois: National Council of Teachers of English.

Engel, D. and Whitehead, M. (1996) 'Which English? Standard English and language variety: some educational perspectives', *English in Education* 30(1): 36–49.

Ervin-Tripp, S. and Mitchell-Kernan, C. (eds) (1977) *Child Discourse*. New York: Academic Press.

Evans, E. (ed.) (1992) *Reading Against Racism*. Buckingham: Open University Press.

Falk-Ross, F. (2000) 'Finding the Right Words', *Research in the Teaching of English* 34(4): 499–531.

Fisher, W. (1987) *Human Communication as Narration: towards a philosophy of reason, value and action*. Columbia, SC: University of South Carolina Press.

Fox, C. (1993) *At the Very Edge of the Forest*. London: Cassell.

Freedman, A. and Medway, P. (eds) (1994) *Learning and Teaching Genre*. Portsmouth, NH: Heinemann/Boynton-Cook.

Freire, P. and Macedo, D. (1987) *Literacy: reading the word and the world*. South Hadley, MA: Bergin and Garvey.

Frow, J. (1986) *Marxism and Literary History*. Oxford: Blackwell.

Gee, J. (1991) 'The Narrativation of Experience in the Oral Style', in C. Mitchell and K. Weiler (eds), *Rewriting Literacy: culture and the discourse of the other*. New York: Bergin and Garvey, pp. 77–102.

Gee, J. P., Hull, G. and Lankshear, C. (1996) *The New Work Order: behind the language of the new capitalism*. St Leonards, NSW: Allen and Unwin.

Gibson, H. and Andrews, R. (1993) 'A Critique of the "Chronological/Non-Chronological" Distinction in the National Curriculum for English', *Educational Review* 45(3).

Goddard, A. (1996) 'Tall Stories: the metaphorical nature of everyday talk', *English in Education* 30(2): 4–13.

Goffman, E. (1974) *Frame Analysis: an essay on the organization of experience*. Cambridge, MA: Harvard University Press.

Goodwyn, A. (1992a) 'English Teachers and the Cox Models', *English in Education* 26(3): 4–10.

Goodwyn, A. (1992b) *English Teaching and Media Education*. Milton Keynes: Open University Press.

Goodwyn, A. (ed.) (2000a) *English in the Digital Age*. London: Cassell.

Goodwyn, A. (2000b) '"A Bringer of New Things": an English teacher in the computer age?', in A. Goodwyn (ed.), *English in the Digital Age*. London: Cassell, pp. 1–21.

Goodwyn, A. (2000c) 'Texting: reading and writing in the intertext', in A. Goodwyn (ed.), *English in the Digital Age*. London: Cassell, pp. 115–32.

Goodwyn, A., Adams, A. and Clarke, S. (1997) 'The Great God of the Future: views of current and future English teachers on the place of IT in English', *English in Education* 31(2): 54–62.

Goodwyn, A. and Findlay, K. (1999) 'The Cox Models Revisited: English teachers' views of their subject and the National Curriculum', *English in Education* **33**(2): 19–31.

Goodwyn, A. and Fox, D. (1993) *Whose Model of English?* Norwich: University of East Anglia.

Halpern, D. F. (1986) *Sex Differences in Cognitive Abilities*. Hillsdale, NJ: Lawrence Erlbaum Associates.

Harrison, C. *et al.* (1998) 'Multimedia Portables for Teachers Pilot: project report'. Coventry: British Educational Communications and Technology Agency, p. 72.

Harrison, C. and Salinger, T. (1998) *Assessing Reading 1: Theory and Practice: international perspectives on reading assessment*. London: Routledge.

Hawkins, M. S. G. (1993) 'Intertextuality and Cultural Identity: a bibliographic essay', in S. W. Lott *et al.* (eds), *Global Perspectives on Teaching Literature*. Urbana, Illinois: National Council of Teachers of English, pp. 264–92.

Hayhoe, M. and Parker, S. (eds) (1990) *Reading and Response*. Buckingham: Open University Press.

HEFCE (1998) 'Research Assessment Exercise 2001: key decisions and issues for further consultation'. Paper to Higher Education Funding Council for England, January: 40.

Hilton, M. (1998) 'Raising Literacy Standards: the true story', *English in Education* **32**(3): 4–16.

Hoggart, R. (1957) *The Uses of Literacy*. Harmondsworth: Penguin.

Hudson, R. (1992) *Teaching Grammar: a guide for the National Curriculum*. Oxford: Blackwell.

Hulme, C. and Snowling, M. (1988) 'The classification of children with reading difficulties', *Developmental Medicine and Child Neurology* **30**: 391–406.

Hunter-Grundin, E. (1997) 'Are Reading Standards Falling?', *English in Education* **31**(3): 40–4.

Iser, W. (1978) *The Act of Reading: a theory of aesthetic response*. London: Routledge & Kegan Paul.

Janks, H. and Paton, J. (1991) 'English and the Teaching of English in South Africa', in J. Britton, R. Shafer and K. Watson (eds), *Teaching and Learning English Worldwide*. Bristol: Clevedon.

Jensen, A. (1969) 'Social Class and Verbal Learning', in M. Deutsch, I. Katz and A. Jensen (eds), *Social Class, Race and Psychological Development*. New York: Holt.

Jones, M. (1991) 'A Map of Reading', in P. Dougill (ed.), *Developing English*. Buckingham: Open University Press, pp. 81–97.

Kingman, J. *et al.* (1988) 'Report of the Committee of Inquiry into the Teaching of the English Language' (The Kingman Report). London: Department of Education and Science.

Kress, G. (1994) *Learning to Write*. London: Routledge.

Kress, G. (1995) *Writing the Future*. Sheffield: National Association for the Teaching of English.

Labov, W. (1972) 'The Logic of Nonstandard English', in A. Cashdan *et al.* (eds), *Language in Education: a source book*. London: Routledge & Kegan Paul in association with the Open University, pp. 198–212.

Lakoff, G. and Johnson, M. (1980) *Metaphors We Live By*. Chicago: Chicago University Press.

Lanham, R. (2001) 'What's Next for Text?', *Education, Communication & Information* **1**(1).

Lankshear, C. (ed.) (1997) *Changing Literacies*. Buckingham: Open University Press.

Lankshear, C. *et al.* (1997) 'Digital Rhetorics: Literacies and Technologies in Education – current practices and future directions'. Canberra: Department of Employment, Education, Training and Youth Affairs (DEETYA).

Lankshear, C. and Snyder, I. (2000) *Teachers and Techno-Literacy: managing literacy, technology and learning in schools*. St Leonards, NSW: Allen & Unwin.

Larson, J. and Maier, M. (2000) 'Co-Authoring Classroom Texts: shifting participant roles in writing activity', *Research in the Teaching of English* **34**(4): 468–98.

Leach, J. (1997) 'English Teachers "On-line": developing a new community of discourse', *English in Education* **31**(2): 63–72.

Levinovic-Healy, A. (1999) 'Children Reading in a Post-Typographic Age: two case studies', unpublished PhD thesis. Brisbane: Queensland University of Technology, pp. 414 and lxxxii.

Litosseliti, L. (1999) 'Moral Repertoires and Gendered Voices in Argumentation', Department of Linguistics and Modern English Language. Lancaster: Lancaster University.

Little, A., Mabey, C. and Russell, J. (1977) 'Class size, pupils' characteristics and reading attainment', in J. F. Reid and H. Donaldson (eds), *Reading: problems and practices*. London: Ward Lock Educational, pp. 86–93.

Lott, S. W., Hawkins, M. S. G. *et al.* (eds) (1993) *Global Perspectives on Teaching Literature: shared visions and distinctive visions*. Urbana, Illinois: National Council of Teachers of English.

McGuinn, N., Andrews, R. and Ashdown, P. (1993) 'Crossing the Divide: meeting points on international literature for sixth form English students and future teachers'. Hull: University of Hull.

McLachlan, G. and Reid, I. (1994) *Framing and Interpretation*. Melbourne: Melbourne University Press.

Maclure, M., Phillips, T. and Wilkinson, A. (eds) (1988) *Oracy Matters*. Milton Keynes: Open University Press.

Mandler, J. and Johnson, I. (1977) 'Remembrance of Things Parsed', *Cognitive Psychology* **9**(1): 111–51.

Marlin, H. (1997) 'Cued Spelling Research Findings'. London: Teacher Training Agency.

Martin, T. and Leather, B. (1994) *Readers and Texts in the Primary Years*. Buckingham: Open University Press.

Meek, M. (ed.) (1977) *The Cool Web*. Oxford: Bodley Head.

Messaris, P. (1994) *Visual Literacy: image, mind and reality*. Oxford: Westview Press.

Millard, E. (1994) *Developing Readers in the Middle Years*. Buckingham: Open University Press.

Miller, C. (1984) 'Genre as Social Action', *Quarterly Journal of Speech* **70**: 151–67.

Mitchell, S. (1993a) 'The Aesthetic and the Academic – are they at odds in English Literature at A Level?', *English in Education* 27(1): 19–29.

Mitchell, S. (1993b) *Questions and Schooling*. Hull: University of Hull: Centre for Studies in Rhetoric.

Mitchell, S. and Andrews, R. (2000) *Learning to Argue in Higher Education*. Portsmouth, NH: Heinemann-Boynton/Cook.

Mitchell, W. J. T. (1986) *Iconology: image, text, ideology*. Chicago: Chicago University Press.

Moar, M. and Bailey, F. (2000) 'Children's Creation of Shared 3D Worlds'. Paper given at the University of Bradford, March.

Moffett, J. (1968) *Teaching the Universe of Discourse*. Boston, MA: Houghton Mifflin.

Morgan, W. (ed.) (1996) *Critical Literacy: readings and resources*. Norwood, South Australia: Australian Association for the Teaching of English.

Morgan, W. (1997) *Critical Literacy in the Classroom: the art of the possible*. London: Routledge.

Morgan, W. and Andrews, R. (1999) 'City of Text? Metaphors for hypertext in literary education', *Changing English* 6(1): 81–92.

Mortimore, P. and Goldstein, H. (1996) 'The Teaching of Reading in 45 London Primary Schools: a critical examination of Ofsted research'. London: Institute of Education.

Moseley, D. and Higgins, S. (1999) 'Ways Forward with ICT: effective pedagogy using information and communications technology for literacy and numeracy in primary schools'. Newcastle: Universities of Newcastle and Durham, pp. 119 and xlv.

Naidoo, B. (1995) 'Crossing Boundaries through Fiction: a personal account', *English in Education* 29(1): 4–13.

Newfield, D. (1992) 'Reading Against Racism in South Africa', in E. Evans (ed.), *Reading Against Racism*. Buckingham: Open University Press.

Norman, K. (ed.) (1992) *Thinking Voices: the work of the National Oracy Project*. London: Hodder and Stoughton.

O'Donoghue, J. (2000) 'To Cope, to Contribute, to Control', in A. Goodwyn (ed.), *English in the Digital Age*. London: Cassell, pp. 69–86.

Office for Standards in Education (Ofsted) (1996) The *Teaching of Reading in 45 Inner London Primary Schools*. London: Office for Standards in Education.

Office for Standards in Education (Ofsted) (2000) *The Annual Report of Her Majesty's Chief Inspector of Schools*. London: The Stationery Office, p. 100.

Pavel, T. (1986) *Fictional Worlds*. Cambridge, MA: Harvard University Press.

Peel, R. and Hargreaves, S. (1995) 'Beliefs about English: Trends in Australia, England and the United States', *English in Education* 29(3): 38–49.

Peel, R., Patterson, A. and Gerlach, J. (2000) *Questions of English: ethics, aesthetics, rhetoric, and the formation of the subject in England, Australia and the United States*. London: Routledge and Falmer.

Perera, K. (1984) *Children's Writing and Reading*. Oxford: Basil Blackwell.

Perera, K. (1987) *Understanding Language*. Coventry: National Association of Advisers in English.

Pilliner, A. E. G. and Reid, J. F. (1977) 'The definition and measurement of reading problems', in J. F. Reid and H. Donaldson (eds), *Reading: problems and practices*. London: Ward Lock Educational, pp. 20–36.

Prain, V. and Lyons, L. (2000) 'ICT in English: the Australian perspective', in A. Goodwyn (ed.), *English in the Digital Age*. London: Cassell, pp. 53–68.

Protherough, R. (1983) *Developing Response to Fiction*. Milton Keynes: Open University Press.

Protherough, R. (1986) *Teaching Literature for Examinations*. Milton Keynes: Open University Press.

Protherough, R. (1990) 'Ten levels of response?', *English in Education* **24**(3): 44ff.

Protherough, R. (1992) *Journal Index: English in Education from spring 1964 to autumn 1992*. Sheffield: National Association for the Teaching of English.

Protherough, R. (1993) '"More Absurd than in Other Subjects"? Assessing English Literature', *English in Education* **27**(1): 10–18.

Protherough, R. (1997) *Journal Index Update: English in Education spring 1993–autumn 1995*. Sheffield: National Association for the Teaching of English.

Pumfrey, P. D. and Elliott, C. D. (eds) (1990) *Children's Difficulties in Reading, Spelling and Writing*. Basingstoke: The Falmer Press.

Quirk, R. (1972) *A Grammar of Contemporary English*. London: Longman.

Raney, K. (1997) *Visual Literacy: Issues and Debates*. London: Middlesex University School of Education.

Raychaudhuri, S. (1992) 'In at the Deep End: English and Bengali Verse', in E. Evans (ed.), *Reading Against Racism*. Buckingham: Open University Press.

Reid, I. (forthcoming) *What Was English? Wordsworthian Framings of Academic Literary Studies*. Oxford: Oxford University Press.

Reid, J. (1977) 'The Scope of the Reading Problem', in J. Reid and H. Donaldson (eds), *Reading: problems and practices*. London: Ward Lock Educational.

Reid, J. F. and Donaldson, H. (eds) (1977) *Reading: problems and practices*. London: Ward Lock Educational.

Robinson, P. (1997) 'Literacy, Numeracy and Economic Performance'. London: London School of Economics and Political Science, Centre for Economic Performance.

Rosen, H. (1985) *Stories and Meanings*. Sheffield: National Association for the Teaching of English.

Rosen, H. (1988) 'The Irrepressible Genre', in M. Maclure, T. Phillips and A. Wilkinson (eds), *Oracy Matters*. Milton Keynes: Open University Press, pp. 13–23.

Rumelhart, D. (1975) 'Notes on a Schema for Stories', in D. G. Bobrow and A. Collins (eds), *Representation and Understanding: studies in cognitive science*. New York: Academic Press.

Rushdie, S. (1990) *In Good Faith*. Cambridge: Granta.

Rutter, M. and Yule, W. (1975) 'The concept of specific reading retardation', *Journal of Child Psychology and Psychiatry* **16**(3): 181–97.

Sampson, G. (1921) *English for the English*. Cambridge: Cambridge University Press.

Schön, D. (1987) *Educating the Reflective Practitioner*. San Francisco: Jossey-Bass.

Sefton-Green, J. and Parker, D. (2000) *Edit-Play: how children use edutainment software to tell stories*. London: British Film Institute.

Sefton-Green, J. and Sinker, R. (eds) (2000) *Evaluating Creativity*. London: Routledge.

Shaughnessy, M. P. (1977) *Errors and Expectations: a guide for the teacher of basic writing*. New York: Oxford University Press.

Simons, M. (1996) 'Picture Power'. London: English and Media Centre.

Sinker, R. (1997) 'Rosendale Odyssey'. London: ARTEC and Middlesex University.

Sinker, R. (1998) 'Media Progression Project: George Orwell School'. London: Middlesex University, School of Lifelong Learning and Education, p. 19.

Smith, B. H. (1968) *Poetic Closure: a study of how poems end*. Chicago: Chicago University Press.

Smith, B. H. (1981) 'Narrative Versions, Narrative Theories', in W. J. T. Mitchell (ed.), *On Narrative*. Chicago: Chicago University Press.

Smith, F. (1982) *Writing and the Writer*. London: Heinemann.

Smith, V. (1999) 'Everyone's a Criminal? Reflections on critical reading in the primary classroom', *English in Education* **33**(3): 54–61.

Snowling, M. J. (2000) *Dyslexia*. Oxford: Blackwell.

Snowling, M., Goulandris, N. and Defty, N. (1996) 'A Longitudinal Study of Reading Development in Dyslexic Children', *Journal of Educational Psychology* **88**(4): 653–69.

Snyder, I. (1991) 'The Impact of Computers on Students' Writing: a comparative study of the effects of pens and word processors on writing context, process and product'. Melbourne: Monash University, Faculty of Education.

Snyder, I. (1993) 'The Impact of Computers on Students' Writing: a comparative study of the effects of pens and word processors on writing context, process and product', *Australian Journal of Education* **37**(1): 5–25.

Snyder, I. (1996) *Hypertext: the electronic labyrinth*. Melbourne: Melbourne University Press.

Snyder, I. (1997) 'Hyperfiction: its possibilities for English', *English in Education* **31**(2): 23–33.

Soskice, J. M. (1989) *Metaphor and Religious Language*. London: Clarendon.

Sowerby, J. (1999) *Extending Children's Spelling Strategies*. London: Teacher Training Agency.

Squire, J. R. (1990) 'Research on Reader Response and the National Literature Initiative', in M. Hayhoe and S. Parker (eds), *Reading and Response*. Buckingham: Open University Press, pp. 13–24.

Stannard, R. (1997) 'Navigating Cyberspace: vision, textuality and the world wide web', *English in Education* **31**(2): 14–22.

Storr, A. (1993) *Music and the Mind*. London: HarperCollins.

Stratta, L. and Dixon, J. (1992) 'The National Curriculum in English: does genre theory have anything to offer?', *English in Education* **26**(2): 16ff.

Street, B. (1997) 'The Implications of the "New Literacy Studies" for Literacy Education', *English in Education* **31**(3): 45–59.

Swann, J. (1992) *Girls, Boys & Language*. Oxford: Basil Blackwell.

Tannen, D. (1979) 'What's in a Frame? Surface Evidence for Underlying Expectations', in R. O. Freedle (ed.), *New Directions in Discourse Processing*. Norwood, New Jersey: Ablex.

Tannen, D. (ed.) (1993) *Framing in Discourse*. New York: Oxford University Press.

Tannen, D. (1998) *The Argument Culture*. New York: Random House.

Teacher Training Agency (1997) 'Initial Teacher Training: consultative document'. London: Teacher Training Agency.

Thornton, G. (1987) 'Language Testing 1979–1983: an independent appraisal of the findings'. London: Department of Education and Science, Assessment of Performance Unit.

Torbe, M. (1977) *Teaching Spelling*. London: Ward Lock Educational.

Trimmer, J. and Warnock, T. (eds) (1992) *Understanding Others: cultural and cross-cultural studies and the teaching of literature*. Urbana, Illinois: National Council of Teachers of English.

Turner, C. (1996) 'Reading and Responding', *English in Education* 30(2): 27–38.

Turner, C., Jones, N., Mitra, J., Moore, P., O'Donoghue, J., Stannard, R., Thornbury, M. L., Tibbits, M. and Warren, C. (1997) 'Reading and Writing: digital directions', *English in Education* 31(2): 45–53.

Tweddle, S. (1994) *The Future Curriculum with IT*. Coventry: National Council for Educational Technology.

Tweddle, S. (1995) 'A Curriculum for the Future – a Curriculum Built for Change', *English in Education* 29(2): 3–11.

Tweddle, S. (1997) 'A Retrospective: fifteen years of computers in English', *English in Education* 31(2): 5–13.

Tweddle, S., Adams, A., Clarke, S. and Scrimshaw, P. (eds) (1997) *English for Tomorrow*. Buckingham: Open University Press.

Tyner, K. (1998) *Literacy in a Digital World: teaching and learning in the age of information*. Mahwah, NJ: Lawrence Erlbaum Associates.

Vygotsky, L. (1986) *Thought and Language*. Cambridge, MA: MIT Press.

Walton, K. (1995) *Picture My World: photography in the primary school*. London: The Arts Council of England.

Webb, R. (ed.) (1990) *Practitioner Research in the Primary School*. London: Falmer.

Webb, R. and Vulliamy, G. (1992) *Teacher Research and Special Educational Needs*. London: David Fulton.

Wells, G. (1981) *Learning through Interaction: the study of language development*. Cambridge: Cambridge University Press.

Wells, G. (1985a) *Language, Learning and Education*. Windsor: NFER-Nelson.

Wells, G. (1985b) *Language Development in the Pre-School Years*. Cambridge: Cambridge University Press.

Wells, G. (1987) *The Meaning Makers: children learning language and using language to learn*. London: Hodder and Stoughton.

Wells, G. and Nicholls, J. C. (eds) (1985) *Language and Learning: an interactional perspective*. Lewes: Falmer Press.

Werquin, P. *et al.* (2000) 'Literacy in the Age of Information'. Paris: Organization for Economic Cooperation and Development, p. 205.

West, A. (1994) 'The Centrality of Literature', in S. Brindley (ed.), *Teaching English*. London: Routledge, pp. 124–32.

Whitehead, M. (1992) 'Failures, Cranks and Fads: revisiting the reading debate', *English in Education* **26**(1): 3–14.

Whitehead, M. (1993) 'Whose English? English and more in the early years', *Chinese University of Hong Kong Journal of Primary Education* **4**(1): 83–8.

Wilkinson, A. (1971) *The Foundations of Language*. London: Oxford University Press.

Wilkinson, A., Barnsley, G., Hanna, P. and Swan, M. (1980) *Assessing Language Development*. Oxford: Oxford University Press.

Wilkinson, A., Stratta, L. and Dudley, P. (1974) *The Quality of Listening*. London: Macmillan.

William, L. (1969) 'The Logic of Nonstandard English', *Georgetown Monographs on Language and Linguistics* **22**(22): 1–22, 26–31.

Withington, A. (1996) 'Transmitters of Culture in the Stream of Stories: two "east-west" storytellers', *English in Education* **33**(3): 28–36.

Womack, P. (1993) 'What Are Essays for?', *English in Education* **27**(2): 42–59.

Woods, C. A. (ed.) (1998) *Image, Text, Persuasion*. Adelaide: University of South Australia, Centre for Professional and Public Communication.

Wray, D. (1997) 'Research in the Teaching of Reading: a 25–year debate', in K. Watson, C. Modgill, and S. Modgill (eds), *Education Dilemmas: debate and diversity*. London: Cassell, p. 4.

Zancanella, D., Hall, L. and Pence, P. (2000) 'Computer Games as Literature', in A. Goodwyn (ed.), *English in the Digital Age*. London: Cassell, pp. 87–102.

Index